Members of the Commission
Chairman: Olof Palme (Sweden)

Giorgi Arbatov (USSR)
Egon Bahr (Federal Republic of Germany)
Gro Harlem Brundtland (Norway)
Jozef Cyrankiewicz (Poland)
Jean-Marie Daillet* (France)
Robert A. D. Ford (Canada)
Alfonso Garcia-Robles (Mexico)
Haruki Mori (Japan)
C. B. Muthamma (India)
Olusegun Obasanjo (Nigeria)
David Owen (United Kingdom)
Shridath Ramphal (Guyana)
Salim Salim (Tanzania)
Soedjatmoko (Indonesia)
Joop den Uyl (Netherlands)
Cyrus Vance (USA)

*In January 1982 Jean-Marie Daillet suspended his participation in the work of the Commission.

Common Security

A BLUEPRINT FOR SURVIVAL

THE INDEPENDENT COMMISSION
ON DISARMAMENT AND SECURITY ISSUES

Prologue by Cyrus Vance

SIMON AND SCHUSTER

NEW YORK

COPYRIGHT © 1982 BY INDEPENDENT COMMISSION
ON DISARMAMENT AND SECURITY ISSUES
ALL RIGHTS RESERVED
INCLUDING THE RIGHT OF REPRODUCTION
IN WHOLE OR IN PART IN ANY FORM
PUBLISHED BY SIMON AND SCHUSTER
A DIVISION OF GULF & WESTERN CORPORATION
SIMON & SCHUSTER BUILDING
ROCKEFELLER CENTER
1230 AVENUE OF THE AMERICAS
NEW YORK, NEW YORK 10020
SIMON AND SCHUSTER AND COLOPHON ARE
TRADEMARKS OF SIMON & SCHUSTER
MANUFACTURED IN THE UNITED STATES OF AMERICA

1 3 5 7 9 10 8 6 4 2

LIBRARY OF CONGRESS CATALOGING IN PUBLICATION DATA

MAIN ENTRY UNDER TITLE:
COMMON SECURITY.

1. ATOMIC WEAPONS AND DISARMAMENT.   I. INDEPENDENT
COMMISSION ON DISARMAMENT AND SECURITY ISSUES (U.S.)
JX1974.7.C5725 1982   327.1'74   82-5973
AACR2

ISBN 0-671-45880-9
0671-45879-5 PBK.

CONTENTS

PROLOGUE

MANY AMERICANS and others across the seas are sorely troubled by the state of the world. Each year problems seem to mount. Here at home we face a deepening confrontation with the Soviet Union. There are tensions with our allies. Soaring military expenditures are not bringing the security we seek. New conflicts arise in exotic parts of the globe, while old conflicts remain unsettled. And over all hangs the danger of the ultimate catastrophe: nuclear war.

There is one overriding truth in this nuclear age—no nation can achieve true security by itself. No matter how many weapons a nation develops, no matter how strong its armed forces become, they can never guarantee its freedom from attack. Both we and the Soviet Union are, and will remain, vulnerable to nuclear attack. The fact is that there are no real defenses against nuclear armed missiles—neither now nor in the foreseeable future. To guarantee our own security in this nuclear age, we must, therefore, face these realities and work together with other nations to achieve common security, For security in the nuclear age *means* common security. This has been the central conclusion of our Commission. On this issue there should be no division between left and right.

The proposals in the Commission's report are offered to Americans, as to others, as a demonstration that people working in a frank and realistic atmosphere can agree on common measures to lessen the dangers of both nuclear and conventional wars.

The Commission is composed of present and former government officials—heads of state, foreign ministers, political leaders—many of whom I knew while serving as Secretary of State.

These men and women have sought to bring to vital questions of national security the approach of practical politicians: what really *can* be done? To no one's surprise, there were strong disagreements among us. After all, we come from different nations and cultures: industrial countries and developing nations, members of NATO and members of the Warsaw Pact, open and closed societies. Yet we found that we could agree on a program of action, on concrete measures which go far beyond generalities. Our recommendations constitute practical steps which, if implemented by the world's governments, could produce a genuine and significant improvement in the international political climate and real progress toward arms control and a lessened risk of nuclear war.

It goes without saying that the Commission strongly supports, and emphasizes the need for progress in, U.S.-Soviet negotiations on nuclear weapons. Among its recommendations are proposals for reaffirmation of the limits on strategic offensive forces contained in the SALT II treaty, preservation of the 1972 ABM treaty, and a rapid start for negotiations aimed at additional reductions and qualitative constraints on these weapons. The Commission also calls for rapid progress in U.S.-Soviet negotiations on intermediate-range nuclear weapons that threaten Europe, and on the achievement of parity, at lower levels, of conventional forces in Europe.

But we have progressed well beyond the familiar items on the arms control agenda. The greatest concentration of nuclear and conventional power is found in Europe. It is there that the East-West confrontation is drawn most tightly. The Commission recounts the reason why NATO and the Warsaw Pact have deployed such large military forces in this region, and discusses the contradictory perceptions of the two sides which make political solutions to this problem so difficult. Even so, the members of the Commission have found it possible to agree on a series of measures which could reduce the danger of war. The report includes a series of practical steps to ease the nuclear confrontation in Europe, to reduce pressures for the early use of nuclear weapons should any crisis occur, and to contribute generally to a psychological atmosphere in which the prospects for significant reductions in arms and political tensions become more likely. In all of this, the Commission recognizes the close link between conventional and nuclear arms control. Progress in neither sector can proceed very far without progress in the other.

When considering any proposal for negotiated arms limitations, Americans are rightly concerned about the arrangements for verification of compliance with its terms.

In this respect, the Commission's report is encouraging. With the agreement of the Soviet member, we have been able not only to discuss verification questions at considerable length, but also to note the specific means which would be necessary to verify particular measures. It is clear that the international community has come a long way with respect to this issue—a distance which makes possible the contemplation of far-reaching measures of arms control.

To an extent, the problems of nuclear and conventional arms are reflections of weaknesses in the international system. It is a weak system because it lacks a significant structure of laws and norms of behavior which are accepted and observed by all states. The fact that nations arm and go to war reflects these weaknesses.

The United Nations must, and does, stand at the center of the international system, but governments have not permitted the UN to function as it should. Time has dealt cruelly with the bold provisions of the UN Charter.

The Commission has suggested certain specific steps to strengthen the United Nations, especially its ability to prevent conflicts or, if its efforts fail, to quickly isolate the conflict, to stop the fighting, and to restore the peace. These measures involve particularly the five permanent members of the Security Council.

On this point, I want to speak plainly as an American. The United States had a leading role in organizing the United Nations and in drafting its charter. Its goals reflect our ideals. Over the years, however, we, along with others, have drifted away from support for and use of the United Nations to contain and resolve conflicts which imperil regional and world peace. It is now past time for us to reverse that trend, to make a major effort to improve the way security problems are dealt with by the world organization.

The United States may no longer have nuclear superiority, but certainly the Soviet Union does not, and we possess and will continue to possess more than adequate military strength to protect our national interests. We have economic problems, but we are also economically the strongest power by a wide margin. And we have a democratic system and values which are widely admired. These factors put us in a unique position of moral and political leadership in the world. I strongly hope that the United States Government can foster improvement in the UN system along the lines outlined in the report.

Over all, the recommendations of the Commission do not extend to a blueprint for a world without armaments and without war. That would be unrealistic. But the recommendations do represent a major step in the right direction. I profoundly hope that they will contribute to a renewed sense of direction and purpose among the citizens of our nation which it has been my great privilege to serve.

Cyrus Vance
May 7, 1982

Introduction: Olof Palme

At the end of the first year of our work, in December 1981, our Commission visited Hiroshima. One of the people we met was a photographer who had been in the city on 6 August 1945. He described the horrors of that day, and he continued: 'It was a gathering of ghosts and I could not release my shutter on such a miserable scene. But I hardened myself and finally clicked the shutter ... After taking a few photographs there, I felt I had performed my duty, and I could not stay there any more. So I called out to these suffering people, "Take good care of yourself", and I went back home. But even today I still hear the voices asking feebly for water.' And he asked a question: 'It was hell on earth. It was an inferno. Was this the real world?'

The Commission began its work in 1980 at a time when the 'real world' of nuclear war may have seemed more remote than it does today. There was also very little discussion about the possibilities for ending the arms race, let alone about achieving real disarmament. The process of negotiating arms limitations was moribund.

Since then, the international situation has become both more dangerous and increasingly full of hope. Relations between the United States and the Soviet Union have deteriorated sharply in 1981 and 1982. The arms race is accelerating. The development of new nuclear weapons seems to suggest that the nuclear powers may actually consider fighting a nuclear war. The threat of war seems closer than for many years. In the Middle East and many other parts of the Third World, war is not a threat but a reality.

At the same time, there are new reasons for optimism. The last two years have been an extraordinary period of popular and political awakening to the dangers of war. Millions of people from all continents – and young people especially – have become involved in disarmament activities. Their concerns have spread across Europe and Asia and into North America. New movements have grown up, such as the doctors' groups who describe in clear and factual terms what a nuclear war would mean.

People are questioning the doctrine of deterrence, of a nuclear balance of terror. From inside the political and military systems, there are voices of warning: Lord Mountbatten and George Kennan, scientists such as Jerome Wiesner and Solly Zuckerman. Governments are producing plans for nuclear reductions. There has been a tremendous outpouring of new and revived ideas for ending the arms race: nuclear-weapon-free zones, freezing the production of nuclear weapons, closing military research establishments, renouncing the first use of nuclear weapons, negotiated and reciprocated moratoria, cutting by half existing nuclear stockpiles.

It was against this background of tension and change that the Commission worked together to produce our report. We were in some ways a unique group. The Commission does not primarily consist of experts on arms limitation and disarmament. Its members were chosen, rather, because of their political experience over a broad field. Many have held or now hold high public office, others have a long experience in diplomacy and serving their countries at home and abroad. Three of us were members of the Brandt Commission, the Independent Commission on International Development Issues. We hoped, in bringing together people of such varied backgrounds, to bring new ideas and thoughts to the subject of disarmament.

Members of the Commission come from East and West, from North and South. They are from the Warsaw Pact and from the North Atlantic Treaty Organization, from European neutral countries, from Japan, and from many Third World countries. They differ profoundly in their views of international issues, and in their political and ideological perspectives.

But each has her or his own vision of peace and security, of a better world in which people may live. And each was also committed to the idea that the Commission itself should reach consensus on a common programme. Each was prepared to make the compromises necessary to achieve such unity.

For the Commission was unique, too, in that for the first time – and under difficult international circumstances – prominent people from Warsaw Pact and NATO countries were able to agree with people from neutral countries on a factual description of the military situation in different parts of the world, on an analysis of the dangers to peace and security, on a broad programme of action to avert these dangers. The process of the Commission's own work in this sense was itself an exercise in peaceful coexistence. Our discussions over almost two years – and above all, I believe, the moving and shattering experience of our visit to Hiroshima – convinced us of the urgency of working together for common interests.

Our report expresses our deep concern at the worsening international situation, and at the drift towards war that so many perceive today. We are totally agreed that there is no such thing as a nuclear war that can be won. An all-out nuclear war would mean unprecedented destruction, maybe the extinction of the human species. A so-called limited nuclear war would almost inevitably develop into total nuclear conflagration. Different war-fighting doctrines are therefore a grave threat to humanity. The doctrine of deterrence offers very fragile protection indeed against the horrors of nuclear war.

It is therefore of paramount importance to replace the doctrine of mutual deterrence. Our alternative is common security. There can be no hope of victory in a nuclear war, the two sides would be united in suffering and destruction. They can survive only together. They must achieve security not against the adversary but together with him. International security must rest on a commitment to joint survival rather than on a threat of mutual destruction.

On the basis of this strategy of common security, we discussed practical proposals to achieve arms limitation and disarmament. The long-term goal in the promotion of peace must be general and complete disarmament. But the Commission saw its task as being to consider a gradual process in that direction, to curb and reverse the arms race. We do not propose unilateral action by any country. We clearly see the need for balanced and negotiated reduction in arms.

Our aim has been to promote a downward spiral in armaments. We have elaborated a broad programme for reducing the nuclear threat, including major reductions in all types of strategic nuclear system. We propose the establishment of a battlefield-nuclear-weapon-free zone starting in Central Europe. We also propose a chemical-weapon-free zone in Europe. Even the process of beginning to negotiate such limitations, we consider, would reduce political tension in Europe.

Many of our proposals concern nuclear weapons and other weapons of mass destruction. But we lay great emphasis on reducing conventional armaments. A large-scale conventional war would be enormously destructive in any densely populated area. There is also a clear connection between a negotiated agreement on mutual force reductions leading to a guaranteed approximate parity in conventional forces in Europe and the possibility of reducing nuclear weapons. Parity in conventional forces opens the way for denuclearization in Europe.

We are convinced that the search for ever more advanced weapons – conventional, nuclear or 'post-nuclear' – is itself a force which perpetuates military competition. We therefore propose a programme for curbing the qualitative arms race through a comprehensive test ban treaty, a chemical weapons disarmament treaty, agreements to limit military activities in space, and other measures.

Our programme does not cover all measures of arms limitation and disarmament. During our work we became familiar with many problems and opportunities which we could not examine thoroughly. We are deeply aware of the complexity of the problems that governments face today in the search for peace and security. We have concentrated our work on areas where we felt we could make a useful contribution to this common effort. For similar reasons, we have not taken up many of the very interesting proposals – such as for a weapons freeze or moratorium – which have stimulated the disarmament debate during the Commission's work. Several of these proposals have the object of achieving a temporary halt in the arms race. Our purpose was rather to work out a programme aiming at direct and substantial reductions in weapons: a downward spiral.

The danger of a nuclear holocaust, which could destroy neutrals as well as belligerents, the South as well as the North, is for obvious reasons in the foreground of the disarmament debate. But the Commission was constantly aware that almost all wars since 1945 have been fought in non-nuclear countries in the Third World. Some calculations suggest that more than 120 wars raged during the first twenty years after the Second World War. The human suffering has been terrible. Many of the most devastating famines of this period – for example in Uganda, Bangladesh, Kampuchea – have come in the aftermath of war, directly caused by the upheaval and disorder of military conflict.

While serving on the Commission I have paid many visits to Iran and Iraq as a special representative of the Secretary General of the United Nations. I have seen at close hand the terrible consequences of war – the bloodshed, the destruction, the horrendous costs for two Third World countries intent on social and economic self-development.

Even the most powerful Third World countries feel insecure in a world of global tension and local conflict, caused by border disputes and other animosities. Their security is threatened by poverty and deprivation, by economic inequality. Many countries look increasingly to armaments – usually imported from developed countries – as a means of trying to defend their security. Yet this diverts resources from economic development and further reduces security. There are moreover some 62 states with populations of less than one million, of which 36 have less than 200,000 inhabitants. They are vulnerable, and cannot possibly afford to build up military strength.

The principle of common security applies with great force to Third World countries. Like the countries which live in the presence of nuclear weapons, they cannot achieve security against their adversaries. They too must find political and economic security through a commitment to joint survival.

We are convinced that it is absolutely necessary to meet the security needs of the Third World by collective responsibility. These needs are closely intertwined with efforts to safeguard peace and improve relations between the nuclear powers.

We propose in our report to strengthen the role of the United Nations in safeguarding security. We describe a programme to improve possibilities for anticipating and preventing conflicts through new collective security procedures within the United Nations, and by an improved peacekeeping machinery.

We also emphasize the importance of regional approaches to security. We propose to strengthen regional security by creating zones of peace, nuclear-weapon-free zones, and by establishing regional conferences on security and cooperation similar to the one set up in Helsinki for Europe. We believe that regional discussions – including negotiations leading to chemical-weapon and battlefield-nuclear-weapon-free zones in Europe – can play an important role in achieving common security in all parts of the world.

In the Third World, as in all our countries, security requires economic progress as well as freedom from military fear. Our report describes the tremendous economic costs that the arms race has imposed on countries from the United States and the Soviet Union to poor arms-importing countries in Africa. These costs are even more serious in the present economic crisis, which itself threatens the security of every country. We share the view of the Brandt Commission that the North and the South have a mutual interest in the recovery of the world economy. Government revenues now spent on the military – and the scientists and technicians and other skilled workers who work to perfect the gigantic military machine – are one of the few resources available to meet social needs and to finance development. The East and the West, the North and the South have the most compelling common interest in reducing the economic costs of military competition.

When our Commission started its work, our aim was to have our report ready for the UN Special Session on Disarmament in June 1982. Our recommendations are addressed to governments, to the representatives of the nations assembling at the UN, to the people who take part in disarmament negotiations in different form.

But we have a larger audience in mind. For the tremendous popular and political awakening of the past two years has created a new public concerned with peace and security. People no longer see nuclear war as something distant and unreal. They see the costs of military spending in terms of cuts in health programmes, lost jobs, lost hopes for development. They know with chilling exactitude what would happen in war to their cities and neighbourhoods, to their relatives, friends, to those they love. They understand, often more clearly than some security experts, the tenuousness of mutual deterrence.

This popular insight is already a considerable political force, and already has influenced events. It is very unlikely that disarmament will ever take place if it must wait for the initiatives of governments and experts. It will only come about as the expression of the political will of people in many parts of the world. Its precondition is simply a constructive interplay between the people and those directly responsible for taking the momentous decisions about armaments and for conducting the complicated negotiations that must precede disarmament.

The beginning of the 1980s has brought an unprecedented international manifestation of concern about nuclear war and insecurity. It is of the greatest importance to maintain the momentum of this period, not to disappoint people's hopes and efforts, to transform their longing for peace into a policy for peace. Our own hope is that our work can contribute in some modest way to this endeavour. We hope that the factual background in our report will provide a broad public with knowledge and insight, that our analysis will stimulate their thought and our practical proposals solicit their support. Our vision is of an international order where there is no need for nuclear weapons, where peace and security could be maintained at much lower levels of conventional armaments and where our common resources could be devoted to providing greater freedom and a better life for people.

I am convinced that this vision is shared by most people around the globe, and I have great faith in their ability to work for its realization.

Common Security
A BLUEPRINT FOR SURVIVAL

1 Common survival

Less than two generations after the carnage of the Second World War, the world seems to be marching towards the brink of a new abyss, towards conflicts whose consequences would exceed experience and defy imagination. Having survived the tragedies of two global wars in this century, wars that touched virtually all nations, leaving tens of millions dead, hundreds of millions wounded or homeless, and a whole continent in shambles, mankind might have embraced new means of organizing the international community, means that could prevent such catastrophes in the future. Indeed, important efforts have been made towards this end, but in 1982, nearly four decades after the Second World War, the inescapable conclusion is that these efforts have not yet succeeded.

Humanity has made only limited progress towards the limitation of nuclear and conventional weapons and has not taken even halting steps towards disarmament. Arms races between the great nuclear powers and between rivals in particular regions have continued for decades and now seem to be accelerating. Every year has brought advances in the technology of warfare; developments which mean that future wars would be more destructive and inhumane. Every year has witnessed the spread of advanced military technologies to more nations. Every year has seen new examples of the suffering such weapons can cause; new demonstrations of man's apparently limitless capability to inflict pain and destruction on his neighbours, even his countrymen. And, most chilling, every year has uncovered new evidence that humanity may eventually confront the greatest danger of all – worldwide nuclear war.

It is long past the time for men and women to halt these trends. The dangers are far too great to be ignored. Decisive action must be taken now to halt and reverse the spiral of the arms race and the deterioration of political relations, and to reduce the risks of conventional and nuclear wars.

Arms and insecurity

Nuclear weapons are awesome instruments of war. Modern technology has radically transformed both the likely character and the potential stakes of modern warfare. Weapons with inter-continental ranges, with flight-times measured in minutes, and previously unimagined explosive power, can destroy in seconds what it has taken centuries to create. Both the United States and the Soviet Union possess thousands of warheads in their strategic and intermediate-range nuclear forces, every one of which is more powerful than the atomic bombs dropped on Hiroshima and Nagasaki. Even these thousands of weapons do not begin to exhaust the nuclear arsenals of the two sides: additional thousands of shorter-range nuclear weapons, so-called tactical battlefield systems, are deployed and ready to be used.

Together with the two great powers, three more states – China, France, and the United Kingdom – maintain smaller but, by traditional standards, powerful nuclear arsenals. As many as ten additional nations may be in a position to acquire nuclear weapons relatively quickly should they choose to do so; one or two may already have covert stores of nuclear explosives.

Nor has the technological revolution ignored the non-nuclear, or so-called 'conventional', weapons of war. Technology has greatly augmented the lethal and destructive potential of all military operations – large and small, regardless of whether they involve the great powers or not. Today, modern jet fighters armed with air-to-air missiles are nearly as common in Africa and Asia as in North America and Europe. Patrol boats with anti-ship missiles are seen in the Gulf of Iran and the Caribbean as well as the Norwegian Sea and the Mediterranean. And modern tanks in huge numbers already have fought in the sands of the Middle East and North Africa.

Together, the nations of the world spend the equivalent of about $650 billion on their armed forces each year, more than one twentieth of their total annual incomes. Three quarters of this huge sum is accounted for by the industrial countries, but military

2

expenditure by developing states is far from trivial, and is growing rapidly.

The persistence of wars and armaments, the dreadful spiral of political and military tensions, and the danger of nuclear holocaust all reflect the weaknesses and limitations of the international political system in which we live.

The hopes expressed in 1945 for a world order in which the United Nations would be the guarantor of international peace and act as protector of states against aggression recede further by the year. Instead, we live in a milieu in which each state feels obliged to display its willingness to wage war in defence of what it regards as vital national interests. Military strength is seen as a symbol of this resolve, but the continuing expansion of national arsenals is in turn interpreted by other nations as evidence of hostile intent, a cycle which undermines the security of the international community as a whole.

This is the international scene that the developing nations, mostly newly independent countries, have entered in the postwar era. For the greater part they have absorbed its environment, adopted its style and, in the process, strengthened its imprint on human affairs. But there are important respects in which the contradictions, dilemmas, and paradoxes are even greater for the Third World than for the industrialized countries.

The sacrifice which militarization imposes on the Third World is of a qualitatively different order from that which falls on richer countries. In a developing nation the decision to add a battalion or buy a warship constitutes more than a mere budgetary choice; it often results in increased human deprivation for the poorer members of that society. In this situation the problem for most of the developing countries is not so much one of disarmament as one of avoiding total absorption into the prevailing military culture and of finding security through other means, in particular by contributing to an effective system of international security in which the burden of making the world safe for all will be shared by all. For these nations as for the rest of the international community, a return to the vision of the UN Charter is not remote idealism but an urgent practical necessity.

The problems of peace and disarmament are thus also the problems of international order. As long as the community of

3

nations lacks a structure of laws backed by a central authority with power and legitimacy to enforce these laws, then nations are likely to continue to arm, in most cases for legitimate reasons of self-defence, but in others to gain unilateral advantage. Armaments are not the only cause of international conflict, and are often its symptom. Nevertheless, frequently armaments are acquired because of the erroneous assumption that security can somehow be achieved at the expense of others.

What is national security?

Traditionally, the concept of national security has been taken to refer to both physical and psychological security, which may be subject to threats from both internal and external sources. Clearly, a secure nation is one that is free from both the fact and the threat of military attack and occupation, that preserves the health and safety of its citizens, and generally advances their economic well-being. There are also less tangible dimensions to security. Citizens of all nations want to be able to remain true to the principles and ideals upon which their country was founded, free to chart futures in a manner of their own choosing. National security also has an international dimension. It means that the international system must be capable of peaceful and orderly change, and open for the exchange of ideas, trade, travel, and intercultural experience.

As we have noted, the perceived requirements of national security dictate that nations maintain military forces adequate to the dangers posed to their security – dangers from within and without. But the realities are such that military strength alone cannot provide real security. By every index of military strength it is evident that most nations have become more powerful over the years. Yet, judged by the increasingly strident tone of international and domestic debates about these issues, it is also clear that greater national military might has not led to a greater sense of national security.

The growth of the peace and anti-nuclear movements in Europe and North America is instructive. These movements gathered strength at precisely the time when many governments were stressing the need for security through expanded nuclear weapon programmes.

The impact of technology

Technology has changed the world in which we live, but understanding of its impact on international relations has not kept pace. National boundaries are no longer, if they were ever, impervious shields, the penetration of which could be prevented by military forces. Populations cannot huddle behind national borders, build up armed forces, and cut themselves off from the rest of the world in order to live securely. In part, this is because of the great economic interdependence of the international community and the ways that modern communications and transportation are binding us together as a global audience to all events. More pointedly our interdependence reflects the crucial technological fact of the contemporary age: *there are no effective defences against missiles armed with nuclear warheads; none exist now and none are likely to be developed in the foreseeable future.*

No matter how many weapons a nation adds to its arsenal, it cannot directly diminish its vulnerability. No known technology, provides, even potentially, a means for the effective and reliable defence of a people from nuclear attack. Thus, one central irony that must be faced is that no matter what unilateral choices a nation makes in pursuit of security, it will remain vulnerable to nuclear attack and thus ultimately insecure.

Technology imposes other costs as well. The advanced technologies incorporated in modern weapons mean that the domestic burdens of armaments are great – not just the use of enormous sums of money, but the diversion of scarce resources, particularly highly skilled individuals and also materials, from solving social problems. Thus, a second irony is that the more we strive for security from external threats by building up armed forces, the more vulnerable we become to the internal threats of economic failure and social disruption.

Both paradoxes suggest that neither physical nor psychological security can be achieved without the development of an international system which would outlaw war and seek the elimination of armaments through their gradual but substantial reduction. This does not mean an international order wedded to the *status quo*. Progress towards economic and social development, the alleviation of political injustices, and the furtherance of human rights must continue. But when nations resort to arms, international society must isolate the conflict and resolve it by peaceful means. Only in such a world will people be able to feel a true sense of national security.

Consequently, if the world is to approach even the possibility of achieving true security – ending the danger of nuclear war, reducing the frequency and destructiveness of conventional conflicts, easing the social and economic burdens of armaments – important changes are necessary in the way that nations look at questions of armaments and security. Most important, countries must recognize that in the nuclear age, nations cannot achieve security at each other's expense. Only through cooperative efforts and policies of interlocking national restraint will all the world's citizens be able to live without fear of war and devastation, and with the hope of a secure and prosperous future for their children and later generations.

Achieving common security

All nations would be united in destruction if nuclear war were to occur. Recognition of this interdependence means that nations must begin to organize their security policies in cooperation with one another. Obviously, this will not happen overnight. But a political process can be started which – if carefully managed and consistently pursued – can develop sufficient momentum to outrun the effects of past failures.

In view of the current global distribution of economic resources and technological potential, to say nothing of military capabilities, implementation of a worldwide policy of common security must begin with relations between the United States and the Soviet Union, and between the two major alliances – NATO and the Warsaw Pact. But the developing world is neither immune to the consequences of East–West conflict nor is it without fault as a contributor to the risk of war. Increasingly, political tensions between East and West affect the developing world, aggravating

6

conflicts between local nations in particular regions. But in some instances, developing nations have played a less passive role, seeking out the political and diplomatic support of one of the great powers, or aiming to gain its economic or military assistance.

The costs and dangers of this involvement are familiar. Competitive arms purchases by developing nations result in the diversion of scarce resources from the requirements of economic development to the military sector. In turn, the contrast between popular expectations for economic growth and improvement in the quality of everyday lives, and the reality of the slow pace of economic development, feeds dissatisfaction, resulting at times in domestic upheaval, and at other times in pressure to divert internal unrest and criticism to external enemies. Moreover, involvement of the great powers on opposing sides of these regional conflicts can sometimes result in a dangerous escalation, the end result of which is unpredictable.

The avoidance of war, particularly nuclear war, is thus a common responsibility. The security – even the existence – of the nations of the world is interdependent. For both East and West, the avoidance of nuclear catastrophe depends on mutual recognition of the need for peaceful relations, national restraint, and amelioration of the armaments competition. But, if East–West relations are to be stabilized and sustained, then regional conflicts in the developing world also must be resolved – or at least their eruption into open conflict avoided – and the opportunities for competitive great-power involvement thus reduced. In a deeper sense, international security also depends on the easing of the present sharp differences in the basic conditions of life in the different parts of the world.

In their quest for security, nations must strive for objectives more ambitious than stability, the goal of the present system in which security is based on armaments. For stability based on armaments cannot be sustained indefinitely. There is always the danger that the fragile stability of an international system based on armaments will suddenly crumble, and that nuclear confrontation will take its place. A more effective way to ensure security is to create positive processes that can lead to peace and disarmament. It is essential to create an irreversible process, with a momentum such that all nations cooperate for their common survival.

Acceptance of common security as the organizing principle for efforts to reduce the risk of war, limit arms, and move towards disarmament means, in principle, that cooperation will replace confrontation in resolving conflicts of interest. This is not to say that differences among nations should be expected to disappear – given the ideological differences between East and West no meaningful convergence can be expected. Similarly, the problems between North and South, rooted in years of oppression and the stark differences in the economic circumstances of the two hemispheres, cannot be expected to be solved overnight; nor can the many regional and intra-national conflicts through the world. The task is only to ensure that these conflicts do not come to be expressed in acts of war, or in preparations for war. It means that nations must come to understand that the maintenance of world peace must be given a higher priority than the assertion of their own ideological or political positions.

Principles of common security

To accomplish these objectives, all countries should adopt the following principles as the basis for their security policies.

All nations have a legitimate right to security
A secure existence, free from physical and psychological threats to life and limb, is one of the most elementary desires of humanity. It is the fundamental reason why human beings choose to organize nation states, sacrificing certain individual freedoms for the common good – security. It is a right shared by all – regardless of where they live, regardless of their ideological or political convictions.

Military force is not a legitimate instrument for resolving disputes between nations
The adage that violence begets violence is as true for relations between countries as it is for relations between individuals. Historically, the use of force as an instrument of national policy has only rarely been effective over the long run. In the nuclear age, it raises risks which are disproportionate to any conceivable gain. Too often, the use of force is claimed to be in self-defence. Prevailing definitions of self-defence must be tightened and

narrowed. Renewed renunciation of force as an instrument of national policy is an important element in a policy of common security. Nevertheless, all states must retain the right to use force in their own defence and, in accord with the conditions and procedures specified in the Charter of the United Nations, in collective defence of victims of aggression.

Restraint is necessary in expressions of national policy
The urge of nations to win advantage over others, to gain security at each other's expense, is the engine that drives the competitive acquisition of armament and pushes the world towards nuclear war. It reflects the false premise that security can somehow be gained unilaterally. Consequently, policies which seek advantage – either through the accumulation of armaments, or by bargaining in negotiations for unilateral gain, or, most dangerously, by the exercise of military power – should be renounced. Restraint should be the watchword of all states: restraint, out of respect for the right of others to security, but also in selfish recognition that security can be attained only by common action.

Security cannot be attained through military superiority
The renunciation of unilateral advantage includes acceptance that any successful effort to reduce armaments and the risk of war would have to be based on the renunciation of military superiority and, more generally, of threatening military postures. This would include the objective of establishing parity between the major military blocs, as well as establishing it as a guiding principle for several pairs of rivals, or groups of rivals, in other specific regions on a flexible basis. Parity must take into account geographic and strategic circumstances and allow for the disparate histories and military traditions that lead nations to place varying emphases on different kinds of military force; adversaries should not be expected to have armed forces that mirror one another in all aspects. It must also be recognized that parity is as much a perceptual as an objective phenomenon. The basic aim must be to establish security at the lowest possible level of armaments. Negotiations could aid greatly in the establishment of these conditions and could help to avoid the suspicion that one side or the other might threaten to ignore parity once it had been established.

9

Reductions and qualitative limitations of armaments are necessary for common security

With parity and the absence of threats established as guiding principles for military relationships, it is equally important that the nations of the world act in concert to reduce armaments substantially. In making such reductions, particular attention should be paid to those types of weapons which raise the greatest concern on either side, as these carry the greatest danger of leading to war. The larger military powers must assume the major responsibility for initiating and sustaining efforts to reduce armaments, but all nations should share in, and would benefit from, significant progress towards this end. The benefits of reducing armaments in terms of alleviating the economic and social burdens of the arms race are obvious. Of even greater importance would be the creation of a political atmosphere in which peaceful relations among nations could flourish, and in which there would be a lesser risk of war.

'Linkages' between arms negotiations and political events should be avoided

Disarmament efforts do not move forward in a political vacuum. They must reflect political interests and the political order and are thus an integral part of international relations. However, it is important not to construct, as a matter of deliberate policy, linkages between particular negotiations to limit specific aspects of the arms race and international behaviour in general. The task of diplomacy is to split and subdivide conflicts rather than generalize and aggregate them. Linking them into broader issues tends to limit, rather than broaden, the scope for diplomatic manoeuvre. Progress in arms negotiations is not a reward for either negotiating partner; it is a means for both to capitalize on their common interest in security and survival.

At the same time it must be recognized that significant movement towards disarmament will proceed only with difficulty in the absence of broader political accommodation. The two interact and must move together. They can aid one another in facilitating progress, but neither can proceed very far without progress in the other. Just as arms negotiations would fail in the absence of political accommodation, so too would movement towards more cooperative political and economic relations come to an end without concurrent progress towards stabilization of the military balance and reductions in the size of armed forces.

Third World tensions

The Third World has been the scene of most of the world's violence since 1945. The cost of this upheaval and destruction has been tremendous. There are many causes of Third World conflict. For most of the postwar period, turmoil in developing regions was the result of the struggle for independence. But even now, when there are virtually no colonies left, many sources of tension and potential conflict remain.

In the absence of a natural basis for the borders for many Third World nations, territorial claims and pressures for the fragmentation of national societies have been frequent and sometimes intense. In many developing nations, historic animosities, religious and racial hatreds and battles for political influence and privilege among disparate elements of society all lead to violent conflict.

Last, but far from least, pressures stemming from economic underdevelopment and the maldistribution of resources and wealth produce stresses and strains both within and between nations. Hunger, malnutrition, poverty and ill-health on a massive scale all work to spur political change, sometimes through violent means.

The developing regions are fragmented and torn by a variety of indigenous conflicts, but many of them have been complicated by the superimposition of East–West tensions. As these tensions rise there is increased risk of their being transferred to Third World regions where indigenous conflicts provide opportunities for them to flourish. Conversely, regional conflicts can themselves lead to wider escalation of tension involving the danger of great power confrontation. The Third World has a deep and continuing interest in *détente*, in curbing the arms race, and in improved relations between the great powers.

Finally, we should note the broader tension between the industrialized nations and the developing world. Politically, ideologically and economically, the North–South dialogue is frozen. The growing economic and social disparities between North and South have been catalogued frequently, most recently in the report of the Brandt Commission: *North–South: A programme for survival.* A failure to rectify these trends could lead in time to worldwide chaos and international conflict. For the present, North–South tensions are mainly of an economic nature, damaging the development prospects of the Third World and also making it impossible to implement long-term economic arrangements that could provide greater prosperity for all. But potentially much more is at stake.

Over the long term, a decline in North–South relations can have the most serious impact on the psychological atmosphere in which we all must live, on the basic fabric of international politics, and on the risk of war.

Common dangers and common security

In the modern age, security cannot be obtained unilaterally. Economically, politically, culturally, and – most important – militarily, we live in an increasingly interdependent world. The security of one nation cannot be bought at the expense of others. The danger of nuclear war alone assures the validity of this proposition. But the obvious economic and political inter-relationships between different nations and different parts of the world strongly reinforce the point. Peace cannot be obtained through military confrontation. It must be sought through a tireless process of negotiation, rapprochement, and normalization, with the goal of removing mutual suspicion and fear. We face common dangers and thus must also promote our security in common.

The destructive power of modern nuclear and conventional weapons, both in quantity and quality, has totally outrun traditional concepts of war and defence. In the event of a major world war, which would escalate inexorably to the use of nuclear weapons, all nations would suffer devastation to a degree that would make 'victory' a meaningless word. The only realistic way to avoid such a catastrophe is to quickly develop a process by which progress towards disarmament is made rapidly, and to establish a system of political and economic cooperation among nations such that all gain an important and equitable stake in its continuance.

In a sense, the truth of these statements seems already to have been recognized by people throughout the world. We are greatly encouraged that as the Commission has met and worked there has been a virtual explosion of popular sentiment in favour of peace and disarmament. It is long past time for all governments to respond to the popular urge for true security. If they fail to meet these expectations, we will all be the victims of their folly.

2 The threat of war

What causes war? The question has confounded philosophers and political thinkers for centuries. Wars stem from a variety of causes: a clash of economic interests, a conflict between political factions or traditionally hostile cultures or ethnic groups, a struggle between antagonistic ideologies, a confrontation between rival nations. But these are not sufficient nor complete explanations of war. After all, some conflicts continue for decades, even centuries, with little if any violence.

There is no rigorous scientific method for predicting war, but we have considerable information about the conditions that have led historically to military clashes. In light of these past episodes, contemporary trends in world affairs are profoundly disturbing. Although the Commission does not wish to appear excessively alarmist, we are deeply concerned, believing that for several years the trends have been moving in the wrong direction, towards a growing risk of war. Unless these trends are reversed, they could lead to military conflicts of unprecedented destructiveness.

Part of the problem is the deterioration in the fabric of international relations described in the opening pages of the report. But there are additional reasons for worry: the intensifying competition between the world's major military alliances – NATO and the Warsaw Pact – and between a number of nations in several parts of the Third World, along with the accelerating proliferation throughout the globe of nuclear and advanced conventional armaments. These developments have sharply outpaced the so-far limited achievements of armaments negotiations. They have greatly complicated some political conflicts and poisoned the atmosphere for peaceful negotiations. In some cases, the arms race is leading to increasingly unstable military balances, suggesting that in the event of crisis the chances of war would be far greater. For all these reasons, the threat of war – even nuclear war – is more ominous today than it has been for many years.

Nations arm for many reasons. Historically, some nations have recruited large standing armies and navies because they planned military campaigns of conquest. Other nations have developed large military forces as a source of international prestige. Most nations arm themselves, however, because of what they see as threats to their security, because they sense a danger to their national interests. These perceptions are sometimes founded on accurate readings of objective reality. At other times, they are the results of misunderstandings, historical animosities, and economic and bureaucratic pressures.

Whatever its cause, military expenditure can have adverse consequences. National resources used for armaments cannot be used for social purposes. Military expenditure can also have secondary economic consequences under certain circumstances, such as retarding economic growth and increasing the rate of inflation.

Moreover, it is evident that the competitive acquisition of weapons by two or more nations can aggravate political conflicts, contributing to a greater risk of war. Thus, the acquisition of weapons can lead to less, rather than more, security. This has never been more true than in the nuclear age. As explained by Lord Mountbatten, shortly before his death:

> the nuclear arms race has no military purpose. Wars cannot be fought with nuclear weapons. Their existence only adds to our perils because of the illusions which they have generated.[1]

An arms race reduces the chances that political conflicts can be resolved peacefully. A nation's decision to increase its stock of weapons is often interpreted by its adversary as a statement of intentions. The deployment of more capable weapons can persuade an adversary not only that it confronts enhanced military capabilities, but also that there is an increased likelihood that its enemy intends to make use of those capabilities. Then the observing state may decide that it must acquire similar or greater military capabilities. The resulting arms competition increases political tension. In extreme circumstances, one of the nations may conclude that war is inevitable, that the balance of military power is likely to worsen in the future, and that it should take preemptive military

15

action to remove the threat poised against it.

Bearing in mind this chemistry of competitive arms acquisitions, a look at present worldwide trends is profoundly disturbing. Military expenditure is increasing both among industrial nations and in most parts of the developing world. Even when this growth is adjusted to discount inflation the trend remains upward. Already announced budgets and weapon sales contracts suggest that military spending will continue to rise for the foreseeable future. If so, history suggests that the resulting proliferation of nuclear and advanced conventional weapons may end in tragedy.

The proliferation of nuclear weapons

The continuing proliferation of nuclear weapons is most disturbing. Since 1945, five nations – the United States, the Soviet Union, the United Kingdom, France, and China – have deployed nuclear weapons; other nations are in a position to do so rapidly once such a decision were taken. The global stockpile of nuclear weapons exceeds 40,000; it may be as high as 50,000.

Increases to existing stockpiles

The primary impetus behind the continuing proliferation of nuclear weapons is the competition between the United States and the Soviet Union. Together they probably account for about 95 per cent of the world's nuclear arsenals. Although restrained in some measure by the agreements that have resulted from the strategic arms limitation talks, the nuclear competition between these two great powers has maintained a stubborn vitality for more than three decades and has greatly complicated efforts to establish a political accommodation between them. Moreover, the pace at which nuclear weapons are being added to the US and Soviet arsenals seems to be accelerating. This is clearly the case for the weapons used in the strategic offensive forces of the two powers (figure 2.1). There seems to be a vicious circle: political tension makes negotiations to limit the US–Soviet arms race more difficult, while the resulting accelerated armaments competition in turn feeds greater political tension. So long as the cycle continues, the risk increases that one day the US–Soviet nuclear arms race will result in war.

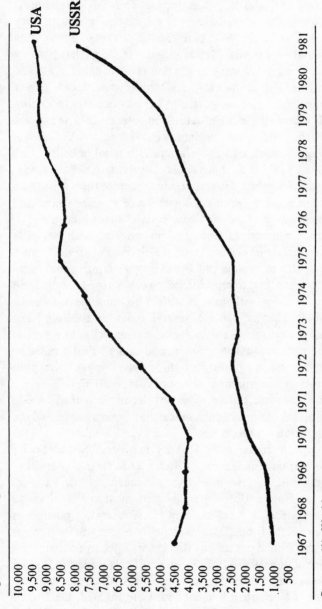

Figure 2.1 Strategic nuclear inventories of US and USSR (number of warheads on missiles and bombers)

Sources: (1) *World Armaments and Disarmament.* Yearbooks of the Stockholm International Peace Research Institute (1969–80).

(2) Annual Reports of the US Secretary of Defense, 1976–81 and *US Military Posture* by Chairman of the US Joint Chiefs of Staff.

17

In recent years, both sides have given renewed attention to intermediate- and shorter-range forces. The Soviet Union is deploying a mobile intermediate-range missile equipped with three warheads, known in the West as the SS-20, to replace some of its older SS-4 and SS-5 missiles. It is reported in the West that Warsaw Pact forces also are receiving newer and more capable models of tactical missiles, fighter aircraft, and artillery which can deliver nuclear munitions. For its part, NATO has decided to deploy Pershing II intermediate-range ballistic missiles and cruise missiles on mobile ground-launchers beginning in 1984. And NATO also is modernizing its nuclear-capable aircraft, tactical missiles, and artillery; some of these weapons could use enhanced radiation warheads ('neutron bombs'), if it were decided to deploy them in Europe.

The other nuclear powers also continue to modernize and expand their forces. In 1980 Great Britain announced plans to acquire new submarines and Trident missiles with multiple warheads to replace its existing force of Polaris submarines. France is pursuing plans to expand its force of nuclear-armed submarines from five to seven, and to replace existing submarine-launched and land-based missiles with new models with multiple warheads. China, which already deploys several types of medium- and intermediate-range missiles in small numbers, as well as bombers, is now introducing its first intercontinental-range ballistic missiles. The existence and upgrading of these forces makes the path towards nuclear disarmament far more complicated.

There are, of course, different views on the question of which side is responsible for the nuclear arms race; the Commission as a whole takes no position on this issue.

There appears to be overall parity between US and Soviet nuclear forces, but fundamental differences in their composition make it difficult to give a precise assessment of the balance. Whereas the Soviet Union has invested most of its strategic offensive resources in land-based missiles, a smaller portion in submarine-launched missiles, and virtually nothing in long-range bombers, the United States has divided its offensive capabilities more evenly among these three elements. Thus, when land-based missile forces are compared in isolation, the Soviet Union appears to be superior. But when bomber forces are isolated, the United States seems to be ahead. Similarly, whereas the Soviet Union devotes considerable attention to air defences, the United States seems to be more concerned about anti-submarine warfare. And whereas US weapons have tended to incorporate the most advanced technologies, the Soviet Union has tended to deploy larger weapons with greater destructive potential.

The nuclear balance has changed rapidly over the years and the two sides deploy new generations of weapons at different times. As a result, the situation can be made to look as if one or the other is gaining most rapidly depending upon which past year is taken as a benchmark and whether present or prospective capabilities are selected as the basis for comparison. These time-phasing differences are used to help justify nuclear weapon programmes.

As a result of the many asymmetries between the two nations' forces, comparisons are difficult. Each side pays more attention to the threats it perceives to result from the other's advantages, while ignoring its own advantages. As concerns strategic offensive forces, for example, Soviet statements at present highlight the US programme said to be intended to improve counter-force and possibly first-strike capabilities as the primary factor aggravating the strategic competition. The US, for its part, stresses its concern about the very large and accurate Soviet land-based inter-continental ballistic missiles which are thought to have the potential to destroy American missile silos.

The spread of nuclear weapons to other nations

Increases in the number of weapons in the inventories of the five declared nuclear powers are known as 'vertical proliferation'. The spread of nuclear weapons to additional nations is described as 'horizontal proliferation'. The two problems are linked in that the more the nuclear powers expand their arsenals, the more likely it becomes that other countries will find compelling reason to initiate their own nuclear weapon programmes.

India set off a nuclear explosion in 1974 which is said to have been the test of a device to be used for peaceful purposes. But India clearly now has the capability to produce nuclear weapons if it chose to do so. Israel is not known to have tested a nuclear device but is widely credited with having developed such advanced nuclear capabilities that it too could have nuclear weapons available within a short time.

Perhaps eight additional nations wait in the wings, the so-called

19

'threshold countries'.[2] These nations have put a great deal of effort into the development of civilian nuclear industries and research facilities. While developing their nuclear expertise for legitimate peaceful purposes, they also have become familiar with the technologies that would enable them to acquire a weapon's capability in a shorter period of time than would otherwise be required, once a decision to do so were taken. Indeed, two or three of these nations are believed to have taken such a decision already and may test a nuclear device before the decade is out.

The effort to slow down horizontal nuclear proliferation has not been without success. It is eight years since a new nation detonated a nuclear device and eighteen years since a nation detonated a nuclear weapon and declared unambiguously that it had attained nuclear weapons status. Even pessimistic observers believe that the number of countries likely to become nuclear powers by the end of the century will be far fewer than the number predicted twenty years ago. Nevertheless, the prospects for a major expansion of the nuclear arms race remain alarming.

The 'nuclearization' of Europe

The US–Soviet nuclear competition is intensifying: not only in strategic forces, but also with regard to intermediate-range and battlefield nuclear weapons. Both countries are modernizing their forces across the board. Neither will permit the other to gain superiority. Unless negotiations succeed in applying brakes to this arms race, the competitive upward spiral will continue, raising severely both political and military risks.

Particularly troubling is the exacerbation of overall political tensions accompanied by renewed attention to the possibility of nuclear war in Europe – the traditional focus of US–Soviet competition. The current situation is reminiscent of the late 1950s, when political tensions ran high over Berlin and when the structure and disposition of the forces on both sides seemed to reflect the likelihood that any war on the continent inevitably would be a nuclear one. What we may be witnessing is a marked slowing of the significant strides made during the 1960s and 1970s towards greater political stability and a lower risk of nuclear war in Europe.

In 1953, the United States introduced to Europe short-range missiles, nuclear ordinance for aircraft, and artillery capable of firing shells with nuclear charges as a way of compensating for NATO's inferiority in numbers of conventional military forces. NATO, apparently, decided to substitute technology for manpower, adopting a strategy that counted heavily on the early and, if necessary, first use of nuclear munitions. The US also deployed intermediate-range missiles and medium-range bombers to European bases in the 1950s. Europe was a convenient location from which to target portions of the USSR in support of US strategic plans. These intermediate-range missiles were withdrawn as intercontinental-range missiles became available in the 1960s.

Also beginning in the 1960s, NATO diminished its reliance on the early use of nuclear weapons. Instead, it adopted the strategy of 'flexible response' and improved the strength of its conventional forces. Under this policy, which remains in effect, NATO relies in the first instance on conventional forces for its defence, looking to battlefield nuclear weapons only as a last resort should conventional defences fail and to deter the first use of nuclear weapons by the Warsaw Pact.

Over time, US nuclear forces in Europe also have come to be seen to be playing a crucial political role. US nuclear weapons in Europe are viewed by NATO governments and by US policymakers as a visible underwriting of US security guarantees. They are seen to constitute a tangible sign of the credibility of the US pledge that if NATO were to fail in a conventional conflict, the United States would be willing to initiate nuclear war and, if necessary, to escalate any such conflict to include the use of central strategic forces. In particular, the development of battlefield nuclear weapons in Europe itself, some quite close to the likely area of fighting, is seen to provide the evidence that, if necessary, these threats would be fulfilled. For the European members of NATO, and also for the United States, this policy is regarded as the bedrock of deterrence and thus is viewed to make possible the development of stable political relations in Europe.

Until the mid 1960s, the Soviet Union had only limited capabilities to strike the United States with nuclear weapons. Instead, it seems to have relied on its ability to strike at Western Europe as means of deterring any US attack on Soviet territory. In the first instance, this strategy depended on the existence of large conventional armies in the nations of Eastern Europe and the western portion of the USSR. But from 1950 the USSR began to deploy medium-range bombers and, in 1955, nuclear-armed intermediate-range missiles capable of striking all of Western Europe. The deployment of Soviet nuclear forces capable of striking targets in Europe, including SS-20s, continued in the 1960s and 1970s.

The role of nuclear weapons in Soviet planning for contingencies in Europe is stated officially by Soviet Defence Minister Ustinov as follows:

> only extraordinary circumstances – a direct nuclear
> aggression against the Soviet state or its allies – can compel
> us to resort to a retaliatory nuclear strike as a last means of
> self-defence.[3]

In NATO countries, many take the Soviet nuclear modernization programme to indicate that in the event of armed conflict in Europe, the Warsaw Pact would resort to the use of large-scale, theatre-wide nuclear strikes. In the 1960s, the Soviet superiority in intermediate-range systems was regarded to have been balanced by the superiority of US intercontinental strategic forces. When parity in the latter was agreed to and formalized in the SALT agreements, however, Soviet superiority in intermediate-range systems was seen to have important effects. This led to NATO's 'double decision' in 1979 to deploy Pershing II ballistic missiles and ground-launched cruise missiles in Europe, and to seek to negotiate mutual limitations on intermediate-range nuclear forces with the USSR.

For its part, the Warsaw Pact points to NATO's nuclear first use doctrine and the short flight time of Pershing II missiles as suggesting that it would be the West, not the East, which would be more likely to initiate nuclear war in Europe. Indeed, the Soviet Union has always rejected the premises of NATO strategy, stressing the absence of any offensive Warsaw Pact designs towards Western Europe with either conventional or nuclear weapons. Soviet leaders, the Eastern side notes, have proposed repeatedly to negotiate an international treaty renouncing the first use of nuclear weapons, and the Soviet Union proposed to negotiate mutual limitations on intermediate-range nuclear forces as early as October 1979.

Despite these positions, the situation has moved directly, because of some changes in weapon deployments and in thinking about the possibility of war in Europe, to a point where there is an increased danger of any European conflict escalating rapidly to the use of nuclear weapons, perhaps even beginning at the nuclear level. In this sense, we have returned to the situation that existed in the late 1950s.

In the event of war in Europe, regardless of the final outcome of the conflict, it is likely that European losses would be unprecedented. With modern weapons technology, the devastation from even a conventional conflict could be tragic. But the consequences of a nuclear war would be virtually unimaginable. Many studies have concluded that even if its intensity were held to hundreds of nuclear weapons, rather than the thousands which potentially could be used, nuclear war in Europe would mean that millions of people would likely be killed at once, and that tens of millions or more would suffer from injuries and from the lingering effects of radiation. Moreover, as with any use of nuclear weapons, the initiation of nuclear war in Europe would introduce the world to a chain of events which it has never before experienced and whose eventual outcome is totally unpredictable.

The deployment of new nuclear weapons by both sides in Europe has raised popular awareness and political concern about the real danger of nuclear war in Europe and its attendant risk of escalation to global nuclear conflict. Negotiations have begun in Geneva to find ways of limiting intermediate-range and medium-range nuclear forces. Success in these talks would greatly diminish these fears and at the same time could make a substantial contribution to the solution of a wide range of other unresolved armaments issues. Additional measures to reduce the danger of nuclear war in Europe are also possible, and are described later in this report.

The competition in conventional armaments

The spread of nuclear weapons has been dramatically outpaced by the proliferation of conventional armaments. Competition among the industrialized nations, primarily between the members of NATO and the Warsaw Pact, is the most frequently cited example of this trend, and for good reason. Together, the nations of these two political and military alliances account for some 40 per cent of the world's men and women in uniform and an even larger share, nearly three quarters, of the world's military expenditure. The increasing diversion of resources for military purposes among the nations of the Third World is perhaps as disturbing, however – if for no other reason than these nations' greater need for resources for economic development.

Military forces in Europe

The size and sophistication of the armed forces of NATO and the Warsaw Pact are staggering; their capabilities are so great that use of the term 'conventional' to describe them is only appropriate in view of the devastating potential of nuclear weapons. Since the Second World War, there has been a revolution in military technology, a revolution which is continuing at an accelerating rate in the 1980s. In terms of their firepower, mobility, and the flexibility with which they could be used, modern armies and navies bear little, if any resemblance to the armed forces of the great powers during the Second World War. The development of modern aircraft and missiles has been primarily responsible for this revolution in military capabilities, but the radical change extends well beyond airpower. Weapons are more lethal and more manoeuvrable by many orders of magnitude than they were in the past. Radar systems, lasers, and modern electronics have made it possible to deliver ordinance with spectacular accuracy. Intelligence systems can provide reliable and detailed data, with minimal time delays, on the size, capabilities, and movements of opposing forces. Computers can analyse huge amounts of data from multiple sources to provide detailed assessments of rival military units. Means exist to move large forces rapidly and to sustain them, in hostile environments, at great distances from their home territories.

These changes have taken place because, since 1945, several industrial nations, especially the United States and the Soviet Union, have devoted resources to military research and development at unprecedented levels for peacetime. A price has been paid for this diversion of scientific talent and research facilities in terms of the productivity and technological sophistication of civilian industries, and also because of the incentives which the

24

existence of such large scientific establishments provide for the continuance of the arms race.

The two military alliances, overall, maintain in uniform close to the same number of men and women. There are, however, significant differences between them in specific components of the armed forces and particularly as concerns the types of force which each would have available in the event of a conflict in Europe. Figure 2.2 includes data summarizing the two sides' military forces globally and in their primary theatre of confrontation – Europe.

At the outset of a European conflict, NATO would have an edge in the total number of divisions ready for combat, but as time passed the mobilization of Warsaw Pact reserves could reverse the balance. In terms of equipment, Western sources report, the Warsaw Pact would have an advantage in the relative number of main battle tanks, artillery pieces, and air defence missiles. NATO's strength would lie in its greater number of anti-tank guided missiles and anti-aircraft guns. As far as tactical air forces are concerned, an advantage in all categories of fixed-wing aircraft would lie with the Warsaw Pact. NATO would have an advantage in the number of armed helicopters. As far as naval forces of the two sides are concerned, the combined navies of the member nations of NATO are larger than those of the Warsaw Pact in most classes of warship.

These numerical comparisons of relative military strength, however, do not take account of the many differences in the performance characteristics of the two sides' equipment, to say nothing of intangible factors like the morale of the two armies.

Nor do they recognize the fact that the balance in particular sectors may vary widely. Of special concern in the West is the balance on the central front in Europe, which, according to NATO, presently favours the Warsaw Pact.

Warsaw Pact countries evaluate the balance in Central Europe as being one of rough parity. This is also their assessment of the overall military balance in Europe and in the world as a whole. In describing these balances, Warsaw Pact nations stress that geographic, economic, and other differences between the two sides, which also have serious impact on their military potential, must be taken into account.

Quantitative comparisons also overlook the fact that each side is likely to perceive its needs differently. The United States sees a vital

Figure 2.2
The East–West conventional balance in 1982

| | Worldwide | | Europe only | |
	NATO	Warsaw Pact	NATO	Warsaw Pact
Total manpower (millions)	4.9	4.8		
Total ground forces	2.7	2.6	2.1	1.7
Ground forces				
Divisions in peacetime	103	210	88	78
Divisions available for immediate reinforcement	n/a*	n/a	8	10
Divisions on mobilization	n/a	n/a	19	89
Main battle tanks	25,500	68,300	17,100	26,300
Artillery tubes	23,000	43,200	9,500	10,000
Anti-tank guided weapon launchers	15,500	n/a	5,800	1,400
Surface-to-air missile launchers	2,400	11,400	1,800	3,200
Naval forces				
Submarines	220	270	190	210
Aircraft/helicopter carriers	20	4	12	4
Major combatants	420	300	320	150
Smaller combatants	730	1,240	660	930
Amphibious units	570	250	410	200
Bomber/attack/fighter aircraft	1,370	510	470	410
Anti-submarine and reconnaissance aircraft	640	300	360	200
Air forces				
Bombers	460	500	80	370
Attack/fighter aircraft	3,830	5,000	2,500	2,420
Air defence aircraft	880	3,990	570	1,490
Helicopters	8,400	3,560	730	160

*n/a = not available.

Based on *The Military Balance: 1981–82,* published by International Institute for Strategic Studies.
Citing this data does not mean endorsement. Soviet data are found in *Whence the Threat to Peace* (Moscow, 1982).

need for sea power on its own part – given its geostrategic circumstances – but believes that the Soviet Union has less of a need because, traditionally, it has been a great land power. The Soviet Union, for its part, believes that its restricted access to the seas necessitates the deployment of large naval forces. Similarly, the Soviet Union believes that it requires larger ground forces than NATO, insofar as it must not only balance NATO forces in Europe, but also maintain sizeable forces on the very long border with China – a hostile nation which also has a very large army. The United States, on the other hand, also perceives needs for ground forces to be used in regions other than Europe. Differences such as these, when combined with an unwillingness to try to understand the other side's perspective, are driving both alliances towards larger and more sophisticated military forces at an accelerating rate. As with nuclear weapons, there are different views about which side is more responsible for the conventional arms competition in Europe.

Whatever their cause, however, conventional arms programmes are unlikely to have meant a net increase in the security of either side. The ratio of forces in Europe has not changed very much over the past twenty years. The main difference is that the confrontation continues at a much higher level of potential destructiveness and with a greater diversion of resources from social purposes.

The growth of conventional armaments in the Third World
Overall, the developing nations now account for about one quarter of the world's military expenditure. In recent years, the burden of arms expenditure has been rising in many of these nations.

The East-West military confrontation is spilling over into the Third World. While the fundamental causes of Third World conflict are rooted in indigenous factors, it is the industrial nations who, at times, act in such a way as to make their resolution more difficult and, for the most part, supply the weapons of war. In 1979, approximately 15 per cent of all Third World defence spending was used to purchase military equipment from industrialized nations.

A fairly recent development is a trend towards the spread of advanced weapons in the Third World. It was not until 1974 that purchases of technologically sophisticated military equipment were made on a significant scale by Third World nations. They have

27

grown ever since. A large portion of the arms contracted for by developing nations has yet to be delivered, however, and an even larger portion has yet to be integrated into the armed forces of the nations receiving the weapons, a process which typically takes several years. As a result, the full impact of this increase in the military capabilities of many Third World nations has yet to be felt; it is likely to be severe. Not only will relations among Third World nations be affected, but also those between developing and industrialized nations, and between the two military blocs.

The Middle East. The nations of this region, including North Africa, account for more than one third of all military expenditure by developing countries. Within the region, Saudi Arabia, Iran, Israel, and Iraq have most recently been the largest spenders.

It is also the Middle East which is the destination of the most technologically advanced weapon systems. Recent transfers of advanced US aircraft to Israel and Saudi Arabia and advanced Soviet aircraft to Libya and Syria represent the continuing introduction of the world's most modern weapon systems to the region. Beginning in the late 1960s, but particularly following the sharp rise in oil prices in 1974, Middle Eastern nations have purchased larger and larger quantities of the most advanced weapons. Today, the military establishments of Middle Eastern nations include advanced fighter aircraft armed with the most modern ordnance and equipped with sophisticated avionics, the latest model tanks and other armoured vehicles, naval vessels armed with advanced surface-to-surface missiles, and all the other appurtenances of modern military technology. Moreover, this upward spiral is continuing without respite. The result is sharply rising expenditure, together with a much greater degree of destructiveness in the war and internal conflicts now taking place in the region.

East Asia. More so than in most regions, the trends in military capabilities in East Asia have a direct impact on the competition among the industrialized nations. East Asia is the one region where the armed forces of three great military powers and one great economic power confront one another directly, leading to considerable instability and potential for violence.

28

China expends more on its armed forces than any other nation in Africa, Asia, or Latin America. It accounts for about one third of all military spending in the Third World. China's army is presently the largest in the world. Although the size of the Chinese armed forces now seems to be declining, they are being equipped with more modern weapons. China, of course, also has nuclear-armed missiles and bombers, which it is modernizing gradually. In East Asia, US capabilities centre on its Seventh Fleet, with bases in Japan and the Philippines. The United States also deploys ground and air forces in Korea. The USSR's forces in East Asia include the Soviet Pacific Fleet, with facilities in Vietnam, and army divisions and tactical aircraft units along the Chinese border. Both nations' forces can be assumed to be equipped with tactical nuclear weapons.

Japan expends relatively little on its armed forces, less than one per cent of GNP. Japanese defence spending is estimated to increase in the future, however. While relatively small, Japan's self-defence forces are modern and capable.

Changes in Chinese military capabilities have a direct impact on Soviet perceptions of its military requirements, as do changes in the forces of the United States and its allies in the region. In turn, both the United States and Japan, especially, have perceived recent changes in Soviet military deployments in the region as posing new threats to their interests, and have justified developments of their own capabilities in these terms.

The situation is further complicated by political and military developments to the south. Vietnam maintains a sizeable military establishment. There are tense relations between Vietnam and both China, on the one hand, and nations in Southeast Asia, on the other. Continuing fighting in Kampuchea at times aggravates these tensions and threatens wider violence.

All these problems are compounded by the continuing infusion of advanced weapons into the region.

South Asia. In proportion to their populations and resources, the nations of South Asia spend relatively little on their armed forces, at least as compared to other states. India has the largest military establishment in the region by far, but spends relatively less on a *per capita* basis or as a share of gross national product than its rival,

Pakistan. Of particular concern is the trend in both states towards more advanced weapons, particularly aircraft.

There is also a danger that the military competition in Asia as a whole may turn into a nuclear arms race.

Africa. Omitting the nations north of the Sahara, the countries of Africa lag behind states in Asia and the Middle East in the acquisition of advanced military capabilities. As a whole, the nations of Africa spend relatively little on their armed forces on both an absolute and relative basis; the equivalent of roughly $6 billion in 1979, less than 5 per cent of the total expended by all developing nations. Within the region, Nigeria, South Africa, and Ethiopia spend the most on military forces and have the largest and most capable units.

Given the large number of internal and international conflicts in Africa, however, particularly the rising tension in the southern part of the continent, it seems unlikely that this situation can last for long. Already there has been a trend established towards the acquisition of more sophisticated aircraft and other types of military equipment. Unless halted soon, the trend seems likely to accelerate rapidly.

Latin America. The nations of Latin America, on the whole, also have been restrained in their expenditure on military forces. In aggregate, the countries of the region expended less than $8 billion on military forces in 1979, 5 per cent of the total expenditure by developing nations, and only 1.4 per cent of the region's total gross national product. Within the region, Argentina, Brazil, and Cuba have by far the most powerful military establishments. The first two countries have begun to produce their own military equipment and export certain items to other developing nations.

As in Africa, a trend has been established recently for the nations of Latin America to acquire more sophisticated military equipment. It is only within the past ten years, for example, that supersonic jet aircraft were introduced to this part of the world. But unless steps are taken soon, it seems likely that the level and sophistication of military equipment in Latin America will continue to rise.

Renewed attention to chemical warfare

A final aspect of the arms race which causes grave concern is the renewed emphasis now being placed on chemical and biological warfare.

These particularly repugnant and inhumane weapons had seemed to be the one type of armament for which negotiations had made considerable progress. Following extensive use of chemical weapons in the First World War, with only rare exceptions these means of warfare were not employed for nearly sixty years. Even during the Second World War, despite the ferocity of the conflict and the development in the early 1940s of chemical weapons much more deadly than those used during the First World War, huge stocks of chemical weapons were manufactured, but not used. This *de facto* prohibition on the use of chemical weapons was partly the outgrowth of the 1925 Geneva Protocol forbidding the first use of chemical and biological weapons, and partly the result of developments since 1919 in the weapons and tactics of ground warfare which diminished expectations about the likely effectiveness of chemical weapons.

In recent years, progress also has been made towards prohibiting manufacture of biological and chemical weapons and mandating the destruction of existing stocks. The 1971 Biological Weapons Convention, ratified by more than ninety nations, was an important step. Moreover, between 1976 and 1979 US and Soviet negotiators made considerable progress towards agreement on the elements of a treaty requiring the destruction of existing stocks and prohibition of the manufacture of chemical weapons. The main stumbling block was the difficult question of how such a treaty would be verified. But in the end, the talks eventually broke off because of deteriorating political relations.

An *ad hoc* working group also has been established within the Committee on Disarmament concerning chemical weapons. In 1982, this group initiated negotiations on the main issues which would need to be solved in order to elaborate a treaty which would eliminate chemical weapons.

The Soviet Union does not state publicly whether or not it manufactures chemical weapons, nor the size of any stockpiles it may now maintain. It is believed in the West, however, that the USSR has stocks of chemical weapons, both of the modern 'nerve gas' types and the more traditional contact gasses. Some Western observers state that the Soviet Union continues to produce these weapons. For its part, the United States reports that it ceased to produce chemical weapons in 1969 but continues to maintain stocks of them. Plans are under consideration for the United States to produce a new type of chemical weapon, 'binary munitions', in which artillery shells or other projectiles would be loaded with two relatively harmless chemicals that would combine to produce a lethal substance when the shell is fired.

In recent years there have been reports regarding the possible use of chemical and biological weapons in certain areas. A United Nations experts group constituted to investigate these matters has failed to confirm these reports (written at the end of April 1982); the group continues its work.[4]

It is clear that existing treaties prohibiting chemical and biological weapons are inadequate, particularly with regard to their provisions for verification and the adjudication of alleged violations. Only dramatic initiatives can stop this aspect of weapons proliferation before it gets out of hand.

If arms negotiations fail

The concrete achievements and failure of past arms negotiations are relatively straightforward. More interesting is the question of how to evaluate these efforts, a question which necessarily must be answered subjectively. To reach such a judgement, we must compare the state of international relations as we know it today, a condition which has resulted in part from attempts to negotiate limits on arms and move towards disarmament, with international relations as they might have been.

One view is that arms negotiations have failed; whatever may have been accomplished is trivial compared to the pace of the arms build-up and the number and ferocity of military conflicts. Those holding to this point of view believe that if the arms race is to be ended, far wider-ranging initiatives are necessary now, and would have been desirable in the past. Indeed, an extreme version of this view would urge the complete cessation of negotiations aimed only at 'limiting' the arms race, so that the absence of false expectations would force the adoption of radical steps to halt the spiral of military expenditure and move towards true disarmament.

A second view evaluates the record of arms negotiations more favourably. While disappointing, these talks have not been without their successes. Their tangible accomplishments are understood to be modest, but not insignificant either in their own right or in their implications for broader relations. Moreover, the record of arms negotiations must be seen both in historical perspective and as a continuing process. Much political and intellectual groundwork has been laid in the negotiations. In some areas, a common understanding of how to approach the problem has been developed, along with a set of principles and procedures that guide the talks. If the necessary political will were developed, these intellectual accomplishments would make possible more rapid progress towards arms limitation and disarmament than has been possible so far.

One way to comprehend the potential significance of past efforts to negotiate limits on arms is to speculate about what might happen if such a process were to cease; if negotiations were to come to a complete halt and past accomplishments began to erode.

The consequences of failure in US–Soviet nuclear arms negotiations

The most immediate effect of an end to progress in arms negotiations would be seen in the US–Soviet nuclear competition. The failure to ratify the SALT II Treaty has already harmed the prospects for further progress in arms negotiations. But both the US and USSR have continued to observe most of the constraints in both this treaty and the 1972 SALT agreements. A clear breakdown of the arms negotiating process itself would have far more severe consequences, almost certainly resulting in accelerated deployments of long-range nuclear delivery systems by both nations.

Effects on Soviet weapon programmes. The Soviet position is that it would prefer to reach far-ranging limitations on intermediate-range and strategic offensive forces, but if it is not possible to conclude such agreements the USSR would take whatever steps were necessary in light of US nuclear deployments. It is difficult to be precise about what these steps might include, the position continues, but in the absence of arms negotiations the Soviet Union

33

may perceive a need to compete in all major components of the nuclear arms race.

In recent years, the Soviet Union has developed several new types of land-based intercontinental ballistic missile. If the arms control process were to break down, additional types could be developed and deployed in sizeable numbers within several years of a decision to do so. One of the older missiles, known in the West as the SS-16, is designed to be deployed on mobile launchers. In the event of the failure of arms negotiations, the Soviet Union could probably also step up production, or extend the planned production run of its SS-20 intermediate-range ballistic missiles.

Soviet sea-based strategic forces could be augmented even sooner than Soviet land-based forces. In order to continue to abide by the terms of the 1972 Interim Agreement on Offensive Arms, the USSR has had to dismantle an older Yankee-class strategic submarine each time a newer Delta-class strategic submarine began sea trials. If unconstrained by negotiated limits, the USSR could simply maintain the full force of Yankee submarines, each of which is no more than fifteen years old and still serviceable. In addition, a much larger and more capable class of modern strategic submarine, the Typhoon class, is under development, and will likely enter service with the Soviet navy within a few years. These submarines also could be added to, rather than replace, existing submarines.

The termination of the negotiating process also could permit the USSR to avoid difficult choices about which missiles to equip with multiple independently targetable reentry vehicles (MIRVs). The 1979 SALT II Treaty contains a special subceiling on the number of land-based missiles permitted to be equipped with MIRVs, and a second subceiling on the combined number of land- and sea-based MIRVed missiles. It also restricts the number of reentry vehicles (and thus warheads) with which each type of missile is equipped. If these constraints were no longer observed, the net result could be a far greater number of operational nuclear weapons in the Soviet inventory.

The effect on US weapon programmes. Like the Soviet Union, the US position is that it would prefer to negotiate deep reductions and other far-ranging controls on nuclear weapons. Until this is accomplished, however, American officials maintain that in view of

Soviet weapon programmes, it is necessary for the US to develop and deploy new strategic weapon systems; this modernization may touch all types of strategic force.

The next generation of US land-based missiles, known as the M-X, could be ready for deployment in 1986, perhaps sooner if a crash programme were inaugurated. The number to be produced and the system in which it will be based are both likely to be influenced by developments in US–Soviet arms negotiations. In the early 1960s, the United States deployed 1,000 Minuteman ICBMs in less than four years. There is no physical reason why, if the negotiating process were to fail, that record could not be repeated or exceeded in the late 1980s.

As far as its sea-based forces are concerned, the United States' prospects are similar to those of the USSR. The US presently is producing a new class of strategic submarine and missile – the Ohio class and Trident, respectively. In the absence of SALT constraints, these new weapons could supplement rather than replace existing strategic systems. The US also could expand significantly the rate at which it produces new strategic submarines and their missiles if it chose to.

The major US response to the demise of the SALT process, however, most likely would be seen in nuclear-armed cruise missiles. These are relatively inexpensive weapons which can be launched from a variety of vehicles. The United States already has a substantial programme to acquire these weapons for strategic bombers, submarines, and ground launchers to be deployed in Europe. The air-launched programme is somewhat constrained in that the SALT II Treaty restricts the average number of cruise missiles carried by each heavy bomber as well as the number of bombers that can be so-equipped. In the absence of these limits, the number of cruise missiles on each bomber could be increased by perhaps as much as 50 per cent. Similarly, depending on the political atmosphere that accompanied a total breakdown of the negotiating process, it might be possible to expand planned deployments of ground-launched cruise missiles.

The overall effect on weapon programmes. It is difficult to come up with a detailed and definitive balance sheet showing what the two sides could end up with. Even in the absence of negotiated constraints, both would have to watch their budgets and would be hampered by the difficulty of obtaining the special nuclear materials used in these weapons. Nevertheless, at a minimum, by 1990 both nations could deploy as many as 5,000 additional nuclear warheads. If the competition continued unabated until the end of the century, the total of additional warheads might be several times that number.

Increase of this magnitude would represent needless diversions of resources that could be used for productive purposes. Still more striking is a comparison of these swollen strategic force levels with the reduced numbers that might have resulted had the negotiating process continued. Estimates made only three years ago suggested that continued negotiations after SALT II could have led to reductions of 10, 15, even 20 per cent within the decade. The net change by 1990 caused by failure of the negotiating process, therefore, in rough terms might be as great as 10,000 nuclear warheads, or 40 per cent as compared to presently planned levels.

The weapon programmes that could result from a failure of the US–Soviet nuclear arms negotiating process could be costly in other ways too. Estimates of the increase in numbers of warheads do not adequately convey the dangers of continued deployment of new strategic weapon systems by the two sides.

For one thing, some of the new weapons that could be deployed would be more accurate and more lethal than their predecessors, and thus could be perceived by the adversary as threatening the survivability of its own strategic forces. This would weaken the stability of the strategic balance by raising the incentives for either side to strike first in a crisis; in short, a greater danger of nuclear war.

Secondly, some of the new weapons being developed, such as cruise missiles and mobile land-based ballistic missiles, are more difficult to monitor by national technical means of intelligence. This means that it would be more difficult to verify compliance with future agreements that placed limits on such forces, and thus more difficult to negotiate such treaties. The uncertainties that would accompany deployments of weapon systems like these could have other adverse political implications as well.

Finally, an unrestrained nuclear arms race of these proportions would add measurably to existing pressures for abrogation, or at least amendment, of the 1972 Treaty Limiting Anti-Ballistic

Missiles (ABMs). Some Western observers have stated that the deployment of ballistic missile defences may be necessary to protect land-based offensive missiles from attack, so guaranteeing the maintenance of retaliatory capabilities. Others believe that the ABM Treaty symbolizes a model of cooperative US–Soviet relations that has failed, and that it should be abandoned because subsequent events have demonstrated the inadequacies of those policies. If it became evident that no further progress was to be made in limiting offensive nuclear weapons, such arguments would gain ground. Indeed, the United States in 1972 stated formally that a link existed between agreements on offensive weapons and the ABM Treaty.

The Commission rejects these arguments. We are firmly of the view that 'The ABM Treaty is not only a vital part of the SALT process, but a prerequisite for... substantial reductions and important qualitative limitations of nuclear weapons.'[5] Anything which weakens the treaty is therefore to be deplored.

The effect on the spread of nuclear weapons to other nations. A nation's decision whether or not to acquire nuclear weapons depends on a complex set of calculations. These include how it evaluates the threats to its security, the reliability of its allies, alternative means of protecting its interests, the political and financial costs of the necessary materials and technologies, and the impact of its acquiring nuclear armaments on neighbouring states. This weighing of costs and benefits will be influenced by several external factors, including the degree to which the nuclear powers seem to be fulfilling their pledge to negotiate reductions of their existing nuclear arsenals. The importance of this lies not so much in the fulfilment of legal promises as in its implications for the degree to which nuclear weapons come to be seen as the stock currency of international transactions. The ability of leaders in non-nuclear nations to stave off pressures from military establishments and other groups depends in part on their ability to point to the nuclear powers' efforts to abolish these weapons. Without evidence, however fragile, that nuclear weapons will not dominate military capabilities indefinitely, the pressures for proliferation can only become more acute.

If the nuclear powers continue to enlarge their arsenals, making no progress towards limiting their growth, and if it becomes undeniable that a comprehensive end to nuclear testing is nowhere in prospect, then whatever moral and political authority the great powers might have had to persuade others to forswear developing nuclear capabilities will be dissipated. It is this political authority, not the system of export controls, inspections, and other safeguards, that provides the essential dynamic behind efforts to restrain proliferation. Safeguards can only implement and build confidence in the decisions of nations not to acquire nuclear capabilities. Controls cannot be enforced against the will of potential proliferators, at least not indefinitely. Achievement of a comprehensive nuclear test ban, which the United Nations has been pursuing unsuccessfully for more than twenty-five years, would represent a very important step to prevent further proliferation of nuclear weapons and to restrain the frightening qualitative escalation of nuclear arsenals.

Thus, if the US–Soviet nuclear arms negotiating process were to come to a complete halt, the system that has been established to control the spread of nuclear weapons to other countries could begin to deteriorate. If the number of nuclear powers, overt and covert, began to rise, the 1970 Non-Proliferation Treaty would come to be recognized increasingly as ineffectual, and the regime of safeguards and export control associated with it would likely be abandoned.

For all their ideological differences and rhetorical bombast, the United States and the Soviet Union do not at present confront one another directly. Indeed, only one generation ago they were allies. Their struggle has not been etched into a history of war and bloodshed that has scarred generations. By comparison, the situation is different in some of the countries that could soon acquire nuclear weapons. Once these nations acquired nuclear weapons, for how long would their use be avoided?

The dangers of nuclear proliferation are evident. Each additional nuclear power increases the risk that nuclear war will occur. The more people there are with access to nuclear weapons, the greater the chance that a human error or the act of a madman could result in catastrophe. The more national systems there are controlling nuclear weapons, the greater the risk of a mechanical or electronics failure that could lead to war. And the more nations there are with nuclear weapons, the greater the odds that one day, by deliberate intent or by miscalculation, someone would initiate what might become the ultimate war.

The political effects. Accelerated nuclear weapons competition would inevitably inject greater tension into virtually any confrontation between the US and the USSR, raising the political temperature to dangerous levels and heightening the risk of war. Thus, their alignment on opposing sides of a conflict in, say, the Middle East would carry with it implicitly a greater danger of military conflict and the use of nuclear weapons.

Indirectly, such accelerated competition could lead each of the great nuclear powers to exert sharper pressures on allies to adhere more closely to alliance policies and to make larger military contributions of their own. This could have significant political effects in Europe, particularly. There might be destabilizing political consequences in a number of European countries and, should events develop which created tension between the two blocs, the danger of war in Europe could rise significantly.

Nor would the other continents necessarily escape these problems. An obvious flashpoint would be East Asia, where there are already signs of an intensifying arms race. The existing pressures on Japan to rearm would be magnified, and if the Japanese did choose to step up their military efforts significantly, over the longer term, the present situation in this region could be destabilized.

Elsewhere, particularly in the Middle East and near the Gulf of Iran, Third World nations could expect greater pressure to make available military facilities on their territories to other powers and to play a more active role in political and military moves of one sort or another. Any conflict in the Third World in which the great powers were involved, because of their supply of arms or simply their political support, would bear a significant risk of escalating to military confrontation between them.

The consequences of failure in conventional arms negotiations
The results of failure in nuclear arms negotiations would be heightened by a lack of progress in conventional arms talks.

In Europe, the military confrontation might be brought to the breaking point. Even in the mid 1970s, when political *détente* in Europe was growing deeper and more stable, both alliances improved their military capabilities on the continent. This raises the question, How long can stable East–West political relations survive in the face of the suspicions and worries that accompany the strengthening of military postures? If nothing else, in order to muster the political support necessary to continue to compete militarily, political leaders might need to emphasize the dangers posed by military advances by the other side. This inevitably would lead to more tense, or at least less benevolent, political relations.

If concluded successfully, the negotiations in Vienna between NATO and the Warsaw Pact about mutual force reductions could minimize these dangers. If the talks were to fail, it would likely have a serious, adverse effect on the stability of East–West political relations, raising the risk of military confrontation. A failure at the CSCE follow-on conference in Madrid to create a new forum to discuss confidence- and security-building measures and other steps to stabilize the military balance in Europe, and also to reduce military forces deployed in Europe, also could have an adverse political impact.

It is more difficult to assess the consequences in the Third World of the failure of arms negotiations because so far these talks have only rarely touched on proposals that would constrain military capabilities in these regions. The sharpening tensions that would accompany the nuclear powers' intensified competition would encourage a step-up in Third World military expenditure. And the aggravation of regional arms competition that might then result would have similar effects. Already there is a trend towards larger and more technologically sophisticated military arsenals, especially in the Middle East, North Africa, and South Asia. This would continue at a faster rate. How far these trends might proceed, and what their consequence might be for increasing the risk of war in these areas, is impossible to estimate.

Is nuclear war plausible?

Decisions to acquire nuclear weapons are justified primarily on the basis of 'requirements' to deter nuclear war. Some argue that the use of nuclear weapons has been avoided for decades because of the existence of large nuclear arsenals on each side. As long as each of the great powers strives to at least match the nuclear capabilities of its opponent, they assert, and particularly as long as each maintains forces capable of withstanding an attack and retaliating with devastating impact against the armed forces and society of the opponent, nuclear war will remain implausible. Indeed, some even argue that this balance of nuclear terror also contributes to more stable political relations, as it persuades each of the great powers to seek to avoid the type of situation in which the risk of nuclear war might arise.

Most people recognize the tremendous devastation that would result from the use of nuclear weapons. They assume that no sane political leader would either initiate nuclear war or take steps which could increase its danger substantially. Thus, in the minds of many people, nuclear war is only a remote possibility – the result of a mechanical failure, the coming to power of a madman, or a similar unlikely eventuality.

Such attitudes greatly hamper the effort to build the political constituencies necessary to bring pressure to bear to halt the nuclear arms race. If people believe that nuclear war is implausible, why should they bother to take the concerted actions necessary to force a change in current practices? And if political leaders believe that the nuclear balance has kept peace between the great powers for more than a generation, why should they risk alternative strategies that conceivably could prove to be less, rather than more, effective in avoiding the use of nuclear weapons?

These perspectives fail to take a number of crucial factors into account. Deterrence based on the existence of large arsenals of nuclear weapons may become increasingly fragile; nuclear war may become more plausible. Three factors contribute to this possibility: first, the cumulative impact of thirty-seven years of accommodation to nuclear weapons may have made policymakers less sensitive to their dangers psychologically; second, technological developments falsely suggest that it may be possible to limit nuclear war; and third, there is a danger that nuclear war may begin inadvertently during a crisis.

The acceptance of the threat of nuclear war
When the atomic bomb was first exploded in 1945, the world was

shocked not only by the destructiveness of this single weapon, but by its novelty. A totally new type of technology had been revealed, developed in complete secrecy, utilizing concepts known only to a handful of scientists. The destructiveness of the two bombs dropped on Japanese cities, widely publicized in official reports and popular books and articles, was seen to usher in a totally new era. War would cease to be an instrument of national policy. And peace would be kept by a system of collective security with some central enforcement authority.

In fact, of course, no such dramatic changes occurred. The atomic bombs of the 1940s were followed in the 1950s by more powerful hydrogen weapons. Further innovations in both nuclear weapons and the means used to deliver them have ensued ever since. Although nuclear weapons themselves have not again been used in warfare, war with conventional weapons has often been used as an instrument of national policy. The international organizations established at the dawn of the nuclear age have failed to live up to the expectation that eventually they would be able to assume greater political authority.

To some extent, these developments reflect the emergence of a certain familiarity with the danger of nuclear war and resultant complacency about the present situation. The tendency is most pronounced among many of the soldiers, diplomats, scholars, and political leaders who must deal with nuclear dangers profession-ally. No person can simultaneously plan for nuclear contingencies and truly comprehend the awesome events which might occur if those plans were implemented; the mind acts to protect the individual's tranquillity by perceiving the reality of nuclear war only in a superficial or mechanistic way. Journalists have written about the shocking normality with which those who deal daily with nuclear weapons on an operational basis come to regard them. The same psychological mechanisms may cause those who analyse nuclear war as a possible instrument of national policy to understate drastically, even to themselves, the potential con-sequences of the contingencies for which they plan. To some extent, this 'trivialization' of nuclear dangers has been replicated in the general population.

There are countervailing tendencies as well. Recent years have witnessed the rebirth of popular movements determined to

42

eliminate the danger of nuclear Armageddon. In Europe and, more recently, in North America, millions of men and women, mobilizing impressive political strength, have demonstrated that fear of nuclear war remains an abiding concern. Indeed, the strength of these movements seems to be linked inversely to contrary tendencies on the part of governments. The more that nations have seemed to be interested in plans to fight nuclear wars, the slower that progress has been made in negotiations to limit nuclear weapons, the greater the strength of the popular anti-nuclear movements. That these movements have already strongly influenced events cannot be disputed; whether they can cause significant and permanent change in government policies remains to be demonstrated.

The illusion of limited nuclear war
In recent years, technological developments have persuaded some people that nuclear wars need not result in global conflagration; that nuclear war could be limited. Continuing improvement in the accuracy of long-range missiles has lent a certain superficial credibility to these propositions, as have the development of nuclear weapons with relatively small explosive yields and the availability of detailed and precise maps of potential targets derived from satellite intelligence systems.

Officially, both the United States and the Soviet Union emphasize the destructiveness of nuclear weapons and, therefore, assert that their main purpose is to deter war by posing the threat of retaliatory devastation. Other political purposes also may be recognized, but in all cases they are served by the existence and acquisition of nuclear forces alone; their actual use is not necessary. Yet, continuing efforts to improve the accuracy and other characteristics of strategic weapons which would be helpful in fighting nuclear wars, as well as public hints of targeting plans and the writings of military officers, suggest that the actual use of these weapons is not ruled out.

Policymakers face a dilemma. It would be irresponsible if they did not attempt to terminate a nuclear war quickly, should it begin, despite the fact that it would be virtually impossible to do so. But considerations of what types of weapon and control system might be necessary in such an eventuality, and the actual acquisition of

43

these capabilities, can make it appear as if a nation is planning to fight a limited nuclear war as a matter of deliberate policy. In short, there is tension between what is best for deterrence and what might help to contain a nuclear conflict should one begin.

Still, this dilemma accounts for only part of the problem. Also, some military doctrines have come increasingly to consider nuclear weapons in their potential role as instruments of warfare, as well as of deterrence. Some military analysts now claim that conflicts involving the use of nuclear weapons, both on the battlefield and against targets deep in the combatants' territories, extending over days or even months, could remain limited. These scenarios envision the 'precise' use of dozens, hundreds, even thousands of nuclear weapons for both military and demonstrative purposes, as part of a politico-military strategy to 'win' or to 'dominate' the war and to assure peace on favourable terms. In all cases, certain types of target, such as large cities, are said to be spared the principal effects of nuclear warfare.

It is possible today to fire a missile thousands of miles and be reasonably confident that it will land within several hundred metres of its target. Even this great accuracy will be improved in the near future. Other technologies necessary for a theoretical capability to fight limited nuclear wars also exist or will soon be in the arsenals of the great powers. These technical facts are not in question.

What is very much in question is the way that this equipment and the people that operate it actually would function in specific situations. Anyone who has witnessed the malfunctions which have plagued all nations' space programmes has seen in microcosm the sort of problem that would have a profound impact on the course of any, even the smallest, nuclear exchange. Moreover, the preparations for space exploration take place under nearly perfect conditions – the most highly skilled and experienced personnel can devote all their attention to a single rocket. There is relative calm and considerable time to double- and triple-check all systems. All this is far from what is known as the 'fog of war' – the combination of uncertainty, misinformation, physical pressures, and psychological stress that accompanies any combat operation. To expect military forces in an operational situation to function anything like as well as a single unit of those forces might have demonstrated in a test is naïve and unrealistic.

Even so, operational considerations are only one part of the difficulty of limiting a nuclear war. To envisage such a conflict seriously, one must make incredible assumptions about the rationality of decision-makers under intense pressure, about the resilience of the people and machinery in command and control systems, about social coherence in the face of unprecedented devastation and suffering, about the continuance of effective governmental operations, about the strength of military discipline. It all strains even the imagination; the mind reels. The underlying dynamic would almost inevitably propel the conflict into larger and larger proportions.

What this suggests is a most dangerous combination of contradictory phenomena. On the one hand, technological trends lend a certain superficial credibility to arguments that a limited nuclear exchange might be feasible. This credibility would be reinforced if political and military doctrines specifying such actions were accepted by political authorities. On the other hand, if such an option were implemented, the actual performance of the forces involved would be far below expectations, leading to much greater destruction of civilian targets and loss of life than had been predicted, as well as continuing pressures for further escalation.

Thus far, one key element keeps these dangers at a relatively tolerable level. At present, there is virtually no possibility that the leaders of nuclear powers could be persuaded that their nation could take part in a limited nuclear war, become the target of nuclear-armed missiles, and escape with minimal damage. Of course, it might be claimed that nuclear wars could be fought solely on foreign territory, but the danger of escalation makes such hope an illusion. One counter-argument that could be made at present is that the cost associated with a presumed 'limited' nuclear exchange, although high, would still be less than the cost of alternatives, such as conventional military defeat. Presumably, knowledge that considerable destruction would be likely – even under the best circumstances, in which reason and technology prevailed and the exchange remained limited – reduces the probability of a limited nuclear option being taken up.

It is the ABM Treaty, above all, which prevents the illusion of a nuclear war with only minimal damage from gaining wider credibility. Without missile defences, the circle of enthusiasts for nuclear options is likely to remain relatively small. If, however, each side deployed significant missile defences, there would be a greater prospect that in the event of an extreme crisis one side or the other would initiate a nuclear exchange with the expectation that the war would not involve the use of large numbers of nuclear weapons, and existing missile defences would be adequate to prevent unacceptable damage to its own society. The ABM Treaty, therefore, is crucial if limited nuclear options are not to become more credible.

Crisis behaviour

Nuclear weapons are accorded considerable attention in international relations. Elaborate theories have been constructed specifying when nuclear threats are appropriate and when they are not, how the existence of nuclear weapons does or does not support a nation's standing in world politics, when it might be legitimate to begin a nuclear war, and when it would be improper. The military strategies of all the nuclear powers specify recourse to nuclear war under certain circumstances. They all have developed doctrines governing the use of nuclear weapons; their military staffs have specified procedures which would guide the use of these weapons; their armed forces exercise and practise these routines. In short, there is now a certain automaticity accorded to decisions about when, where, and how nuclear weapons would be used.

On more than one occasion, the danger of nuclear war has arisen because an international situation has developed in which one or both of the great nuclear powers indicated a preparedness to escalate the confrontation beyond the nuclear threshold. Such actions – sometimes only verbal statements, but on other occasions involving movements in the disposition of nuclear forces – typically have been undertaken to underline that one of the powers sees a vital stake in the situation, thus adding credibility to its demands and reassurance to its allies.

It is claimed that there have been around thirty such incidents, involving either the United States or the Soviet Union or both, and in one instance the United Kingdom. But some of these were only routine precautionary measures initiated by low-level staffs. Moreover, the majority of them took place in the 1950s, when there were somewhat more cavalier attitudes to the utterance of nuclear threats. Still, in 1962, the world held its breath as the US and USSR confronted one another over Cuba. And, as recently as 1973, during the Arab–Israeli War, a number of steps indicated that serious preparations were being taken for the possible use of nuclear forces.

Any such incident could get out of hand. The way that governments typically make decisions under pressure deviates considerably from models envisioning the rational contemplation of events and careful evaluation of alternatives. The information available is almost always sketchy and inconsistent, if not downright contradictory. Domestic pressures typically militate for action, any action, and they are considerable. A failure to act is seen to exhibit a lack of will, weakness, and resolve. The government bureaucracy continues to pursue familiar routines and existing plans, rarely being able to adapt to the subtleties of changing circumstances. Moreover, the inner core of decision-makers is vulnerable to peculiar group dynamics, making them susceptible to ideas which in calmer times would be quickly dismissed.

When contemplating images of nuclear war, we are entering a realm beyond human experience. There would be no benchmarks to guide action. Indeed, no words are vivid enough to describe what such a situation might be like.

Most important, as history has too often witnessed, international disasters frequently are the consequence of decisions taken piecemeal. Had decision-makers known what the end result might have been, undoubtedly they would have chosen alternative courses of action. Instead, faced with a loss of some magnitude, they took a small step, admittedly with some short-term risk, but also with the prospect of rectifying the situation. When that first step failed to correct the problem, however, the decision-makers then faced a choice between losing a now significant investment of prestige and political capital or taking a second step with a greater element of risk. And so it goes on.

A good example of how nuclear war might start is the 1973 situation in the Middle East. As war between Israel, on the one hand, and Egypt and Syria, on the other, continued over a period of weeks, both the United States and the Soviet Union became increasingly drawn in. Finally, the danger arose that the situation might have evolved into a nuclear conflict.

Fortunately, the 1973 confrontation was resolved without actual combat between the great powers. But what if it had not? What if the crisis had taken place not during a period of *détente* and uninterrupted negotiations and dialogue at the highest levels, when relative calm pervaded their overall relations, but at a time, like the present, when tension and suspicion dominate? What if the chain of events had continued to escalate and the armed forces of the two great nuclear powers had begun to fire at one another? How would the conflict have been brought to a close? At each decision point the risk of further escalation, even including the possibility of nuclear combat, could appear to be less dangerous than the known political costs of yielding to the adversary. Thus, step by step, the two sides could enter a process which could lead to the first rupture of the 37-year-old barrier against the use of nuclear weapons. And once that threshold is crossed, the world enters the unknown.

3 The consequences of war

Nuclear weapons have changed the world. The dropping of atomic bombs on Hiroshima and Nagasaki in August 1945 posed the questions, Would mankind survive as the dominant species of the planet earth? Or would he eventually destroy himself and all of his works?

The development of nuclear weapons has forced a re-examination of the meaning of security and the basic purposes of foreign and defence policies. Apart from their traditional objectives of protecting and enhancing national interests, these policies now have to accommodate an additional and over-riding goal – avoiding nuclear war. For there is no defence against missiles armed with nuclear warheads. The only way to withstand nuclear war is to prevent it from occurring.

Ironically, despite their intense ideological and political struggle, fear of nuclear war has enabled NATO and the Warsaw Pact to confront one another for nearly four decades without direct combat. Still, it would require a great leap of faith to believe that an uneasy peace based on the threat of nuclear devastation could persist indefinitely. There is reason to believe that the deterrence of nuclear war is becoming increasingly fragile. And, in any event, fear of nuclear war has not been sufficient to keep the peace in the Third World. More than 100 wars have been fought in Africa, Asia, and Latin America since the dawn of the nuclear age, resulting in innumerable premature and senseless deaths and, indirectly, in the death or tremendous suffering of countless others. Moreover, technological advances in the capabilities of conventional weapons and their use by an increasing number of nations brings greater destructiveness and higher casualties each time violence flares. Renewed attention to chemical and biological weapons raises the prospect that future 'conventional' wars would be even more inhumane.

Discussions of the danger of nuclear war and of conventional conflicts utilizing advanced weaponry are hampered by the fact that the phenomena are outside common experience. Most of us are unfamiliar with these weapons and the consequences of their use. We know that future wars would be terribly destructive, in the nuclear case exceeding all past experience, but it is difficult to comprehend their true horror. Only when men and women are able to look these calamities straight in the eye, only when they truly understand the utter destructiveness and inhumanity of modern warfare, are they likely to take the steps necessary to prevent future tragedies.

Nuclear war

When a nuclear weapon explodes in the atmosphere, the first noticeable effect is a blinding flash of intense white light strong enough to blind observers many kilometres away. The light does not kill, but the heat that come with it does. Both light and heat are emitted by the 'fireball' caused by the explosion, a mass of air containing the residues of the weapon, heated to the order of 10 million degrees centigrade. Any unprotected person within two kilometres of the fireball will be killed by the heat alone. With a weapon of low yield, say 10 to 20 kilotons, roughly the size of the bombs dropped on the Japanese cities, second-degree burns will be suffered as far as three kilometres from the explosion.

Within seconds, the light and heat are followed by a blast wave. It arrives like a thunderclap, pursued by hurricane-force winds strong enough to uproot telephone poles and trees, overturn trucks, and sweep human beings along at a tremendous speed. The compression of air pressure brought on by the wind and the blast wave itself will crush buildings, killing nearly everyone inside, and loosen bricks and paving stones which will hurtle in all directions, knocking over everything in their path. Anyone in the open or in ordinary buildings within 1.5 kilometres of the blast will have virtually no chance of surviving.

As the fireball rises, it cools and becomes a cloud, hovering high off the ground. Beneath it, a column of dust and smoke is sucked up from below. Looking like an enormous mushroom, six kilometres high and four across, the cloud is a mass of radioactive atoms, some of which are lethal enough to kill anyone who had managed to survive the heat and blast effects.

If the explosion occurs close to the ground, the immediate effects will be greater, as thousands of tons of radioactive soil are sucked into the air in deadly concentrations and deposited over a wide area. Although its deadliness dissipates rapidly, harmful radioactive materials from the blast can be carried thousands of miles and not reach the ground for weeks. Over the decades to follow, the risk of cancer and, possibly, genetic defects will be great. Neither the unborn nor the unconceived can escape the effects of nuclear war.

These are only the direct effects of a nuclear explosion; secondary destruction will be ubiquitous and intense. Fires will be the worst hazard, caused both by the heat of the explosion and by falling debris, broken gas mains, ruptured fuel tanks, and the like. Under certain circumstances, the fires triggered by the blast will coalesce, forming a storm of heat and flame that will ravage huge areas and be virtually impossible to extinguish until there are no more materials to feed on. Other secondary effects will also be devastating. The destruction of water mains and sewers will result in the spread of infectious diseases in epidemic proportions. Communications and other electronic systems will be disrupted severely by the electromagnetic pulse emitted by the blast. The damage from blown transformers and overloaded computing and switching circuits will be extensive and difficult to repair. As a result, the allocation of emergency equipment, even the identification of the location of injuries and damage, will be difficult. And finally, the deaths of doctors and other medical personnel, and the destruction of health care facilities and other municipal services, will mean that even minor injuries and common diseases will result in many more deaths than normally would be expected.

The exact consequences of an exchange of nuclear weapons would depend on many factors. Among the most important would be the weather; winter would be a particularly cruel time for those few who managed to survive. But the overriding influence would be the number of bombs used and the extent of the attacks. A nation's ability to contain the effects of a single explosion would depend greatly on whether or not the central government could shift people, water, food, and medical supplies from other regions. If the war were widespread, its effects could well be synergistic; that is, the cumulative results of burns, blast injuries, radiation disease, and secondary consequences such as the spread of infectious diseases could be far greater than the sum of their individual effects.

At some point, a nuclear exchange could bring urban civilization to an end. It is difficult to imagine the continuance of social discipline in the face of the devastation that would accompany a war involving hundreds, much less thousands, of nuclear explosions. Would people be willing to abide by the authority of a government that had just led its country to incredible disaster? If not, the basic services upon which modern society depends – such as protection from criminal elements, the banking and monetary system, the generation and distribution of electric power, the distribution of water and food to urban areas – could well come to a halt. Society could regress to autonomous bands of people living largely in the rural areas that had been spared the worst radiation, each surviving primitively on its own wits and resources.

Jonathan Schell has put it well, in *The Fate of the Earth* (first published in the *New Yorker,* February 1982):

> [Although nuclear strategists] speak of a period of 'recovery' after a limited attack, the likelier prospect is a long-term radical deterioration in the conditions of life ... To restore [these] essentials of life takes time; but there would be no time. Hunger, illness, and possibly cold would press in on the dazed, bewildered, disorganized, injured remnant of the population on the very day of the attack. They would have to start foraging immediately for their next meal. Sitting among the debris of the Space Age, they would find that the pieces of a shattered modern economy around them ... were mismatched to their elemental needs.

Looking into the future, considering the potential long-term effects of many nuclear explosions on the human gene pool and the incidence of cancer, to say nothing of its likely effects on the ozone layer and resultant destruction of animal and plant life and eventual climatic changes, human life itself could be in jeopardy. Thus, humanity would face the ultimate risk – its own extinction.[6]

Effects of nuclear attacks on urban areas

Within five years of the nuclear explosion in Hiroshima two hundred thousand people had died from the effects of the bomb. Within a similar period of time, fatalities attributable to the nuclear blast in Nagasaki, where the hilly topography of the city tended to limit its effects, rose to 140,000. Even today, the death toll is still rising in both cities, albeit slowly, as such long-term effects as an increasing cancer rate continue to manifest themselves.[7]

Every year, the descendants of those who died at Hiroshima light lanterns, each one inscribed with the names of a dead family. They push the lights off into the river that runs through the city. For miles, the whole river appears to be one mass of flame.

And what of the survivors? In December 1981, the Commission visited Hiroshima and spoke with survivors of the atomic bomb. Consider the testimony of Mr Yoshiaki Fukahori, a survivor of the Nagasaki bomb:

> Some people say that the survivors are more fortunate than those who died, but is that really so? Those of us who have survived these thirty-six years having to fight to find food, to find clothes, to find a livelihood ... I rather think that we are suffering from a heavier cross ... Because I was young when I was exposed to radiation, I have a tremendous uncertainty about the future of my health. My wife is also a victim and is suffering from disease ... As parents we are uncertain about the future of our children, the second generation victims ... Would my children be able to father and mother healthy children? Would the third generation of my family survive?[8]

Projecting the consequences of a nuclear explosion for a modern urban area on the basis of the bombs exploded over Japanese cities in 1945 is tricky. Nuclear weapons have changed tremendously. The bombs used against Japan are relatively small by current standards, and the distribution of the energy released by the explosions among light, heat, blast, and radioactive emissions is likely to be different in modern bombs. The characteristics of cities also have changed. The Japanese cities of the 1940s, constructed largely of wood, probably suffered much more from fire than would modern cities. On the other hand, the Japanese cities had relatively small populations by contemporary standards, and thus suffered fewer casualties than might occur today.

Still, fairly reliable estimates can and have been made. The US Office of Technology Assessment, for one, has analysed several hypothetical examples of single nuclear bombs dropped on modern cities. Consider, for example, the effects of a one-megaton weapon, the equivalent of one million tons of conventional explosives, roughly the size of the warhead of a US Minuteman II or Soviet SS-11 ICBM, on the cities of Detroit and Leningrad, each with populations of about four million.

If the weapon exploded in the air over Detroit at night, without warning, approximately 470,000 people would be killed, and another 630,000 injured. If the same weapon were exploded during the daytime, when the downtown part of the city was crowded with commuters, an additional 130,000 would die. A one-megaton weapon exploded over Leningrad would be even more devastating, as the population of that city is less suburban and more closely packed. Under the same night-time conditions specified for the Detroit estimate, 890,000 residents of Leningrad would be killed, and another 1,260,000 injured. More than one half the city's total population would be the victims of a single nuclear explosion.

Large warheads like the one just described, however, are going out of fashion. The nuclear powers have been replacing their existing weapons with yields in the megaton range with greater numbers of weapons with smaller explosive yields. These smaller weapons are more efficient. Several kiloton-range weapons can do greater damage, even though their total yield may be less than a single-megaton weapon. For example, the detonation of ten 40-kiloton weapons over Leningrad, in aggregate only 40 per cent the yield of a single one-megaton weapon, would likely result in 130,000 additional fatalities.

The physical devastation in either city would be incredible. Houses would be demolished or made uninhabitable in an area of more than 300 square kilometres. If the bomb were exploded on the surface, an area extending well beyond either city's municipal boundaries (more than 1,000 square kilometres) would be contaminated by radiation. Rescue workers and medical personnel could enter this zone to help the injured only at the peril of their own lives.

Radiation dangers aside, rescue work would be extraordinarily difficult. Fires would rage, water mains would flood, power lines would be down, bridges, freeways, and elevated railroads would have collapsed. Once proud cities would be reduced to debris.

The effects of a nuclear explosion on the medical treatment system would be particularly devastating. The Commission met separately with Drs Howard Hiatt and Eugene Chazov, US and Soviet leaders, respectively, of an international movement of physicians concerned about the danger of nuclear war. Their testimony makes clear that it would be impossible to provide modern medical assistance, even basic care, to the victims of a nuclear attack.

John Hersey recorded the effects of the 1945 explosion on the Hiroshima health care system:

> Of 150 doctors in the city, 65 were already dead and most of the rest were wounded; of 1,780 nurses, 1,654 were dead or too badly hurt to work. In the biggest hospital, that of the Red Cross, only 6 doctors out of 30 were able to function, and only 10 nurses out of more than 200.[9]

Yet numbers and statistical estimates cannot begin to convey the horror of nuclear war, nor the grisly consequences of the destruction of the medical system. Consider the testimony before the Commission of Dr Tatsuichiro Akizuki, a physician associated with the St Franciscan Hospital in Nagasaki:

> Our hospital was at a point 1.5 kilometers from hypocenter, therefore the patients and we suffered from only minor injuries. But the building was burned down several hours later. From the burning city, grotesque looking naked people came in droves and they moaned in agony and pain. It took time for me to realize that they were human beings suffering from severe burns and bruises ... All the major hospitals were burned down or collapsed, and most of the victims died without receiving any treatment. Several hundred people came to me. They were turning black and purple, vomiting blood and passing black stools before they died. These were the symptoms of acute radiation illness ... There was a big hospital thirty kilometers away, but there was no means to

go there. Tens of thousands of people died without receiving any treatment ... Patients lay in holes dug in the ground, and people died one after another because of radiation illness ... I felt helpless as a doctor. I could not give any treatment to the survivors ... What would happen if a nuclear war should occur now? Even if you have doctors, even if you have medicines, human beings are helpless. No matter how much medicine has improved, medicine is helpless in the face of atomic war. It was actually a hell, an inferno.[10]

It is clear that the number of people who might ultimately survive a nuclear attack, to say nothing of the physical recovery of the devastated area, would be crucially dependent upon help from the outside. But what if the attack were not an isolated one against a single city? What if tens, or hundreds of major metropolitan areas were devastated by nuclear weapons? If this happened the chances for rebuilding anything resembling our present society would be slim.

The chaos that would accompany such an attack is almost inconceivable. Even if only a handful of cities were struck initially, it would cause an overwhelming panic. Every urban dweller would assume that his city would be the next target, turmoil would come as people fled to the countryside. In some regions, like the American West, many refugees could be accommodated. In areas like the American Northeast, however, or most parts of the Soviet Union, during winter, the evacuations of cities would have terrible consequences. Winds would spread the fall-out over crop lands and river basins. What would be safe to eat, or to drink? In some regions the urban evacuees would be met by a hostile rural population. Even the central political authorities, to the extent that they survived, would be uncertain about the status or well-being of other parts of the country.

The reports from Hiroshima and Nagasaki reveal that the instinctive reaction of many of the victims was to protect themselves by leaving the bombed areas as quickly as possible. Children abandoned parents, husbands left wives. Only one bond remained intact – mothers would not be parted from their children. Undoubtedly, amid this disturbance and upheaval, some would find unknown sources of strength and character. But would this be

56

enough to resist the general chaos, to counter the terror of those whose lives and minds had been torn asunder, first by the explosions themselves, and later by the after-effects of illness, disfigurement, insecurity, and the destruction of family, home, and everything familiar?

There is no satisfactory way to answer this question. But official US estimates of American fatalities in the event of a large-scale nuclear attack, assuming no effective measures of civil defence, range from 105 to 165 million. Comparable estimates of Soviet fatalities range between 50 and 100 million. In both cases, it can be assumed that virtually the entire economic infrastructure would have been destroyed. Under such conditions, those who optimistically predict a return to ordinary life within one generation are naïve. More realistic is the conclusion by the US Office of Technology Assessment that a nuclear attack involving thousands of warheads, 'would place in question whether the United States (or the Soviet Union) would ever recover its position as an organized, workable, and powerful country'.

A meeting of distinguished doctors from East and West was more pessimistic. They concluded that an all-out nuclear exchange between the United States and the Soviet Union would immediately kill some 200 million men, women, and children. Sixty million more would be injured, of whom 30 million would suffer from radiation sickness, 20 million would experience trauma and burns, and another 10 million would be affected by all three afflictions.

At the same time, 80 per cent of the doctors would have been killed and a similar percentage of hospital beds destroyed. Stores of blood plasma, morphine, antibiotics, and intravenous fluids also would have been destroyed. The report concluded:

> The fabric of society would disintegrate and the medical care system, deprived of the facilities developed over the years, would revert to the level of earlier centuries. The surviving walking wounded, physicians and laymen alike, could only provide what mutual comfort the remnants of their individual humanity would permit. The earth will be seared, the skies heavy with lethal concentrations of radioactive particles, and no response to medical needs can be expected from medicine.[11]

Not only would the US and USSR suffer. For example, climatic changes would be likely. The vast amount of polluting dust drawn into the atmosphere would cool the air by as much as one degree centigrade. A large proportion of the world's wheat stocks are kept at high latitudes. If these stocks were destroyed and the American, Canadian and Russian farmlands contaminated, many countries would suffer famine on a wide scale.

More than this, the supply of agricultural machinery, pesticides, and fertilizers that now are exported by the industrialized countries would cease. The fruits of agricultural research would no longer be available. For many Third World countries, crop yields would fall dramatically, turning even those countries that are presently self-sufficient into nations with a potential for famine.

The world in the 1980s is far more complex than it was even a generation ago. Trade has grown rapidly, interdependence is intimate and ubiquitous. Without the ability to sell oil and other raw materials, textiles and machinery, without being able to import trucks, tractors, tools, fuel, and pharmaceuticals, industry and agriculture in the developing nations would grind to a halt. In many areas, the developing world is like Europe a generation ago, with large urban populations and complex industrial needs. Without trade it would sink. Without the fabric of international financial exchange, all nations, both rich and poor, developed and developing, would shrink to subsistence.

In a world undergoing such fast, tumultuous and all-embracing destruction it would be difficult for any society to avoid its consequences. One cannot guess at the degree of social and political disruption, and the breakdown of communications would only add to rumour, feeding the seeds of fear, breeding despair and changing human life in a way and at a speed that is almost unimaginable.

No past war can help us understand the impact of a nuclear war. In the Second World War, despite the astronomical death-toll and appalling barbarism, there was no massive breakdown of society or morale. Air raids on cities and industries rarely caused damage and disruption that could not be bypassed in a few days. Individuals suffered, of course, but for many 'life laughed and moved on unsubdued'. An all-out nuclear war would create a degree of chaos and confusion for which humanity is totally

58

unprepared, and for which it can never prepare. It could mean the end of life itself.

Effects of nuclear wars 'limited' to military targets

Recently considerable attention has been focused on the possibility of fighting nuclear wars whose effects would be confined to military targets. Developments in the technology of nuclear weapons and the systems used to target, control, and deliver them have convinced some people that such nuclear wars are feasible, and that they could be fought with only relatively minor losses to the civilian population. This development is one of several threatening to make nuclear war more plausible.

In reality, any use of nuclear weapons would carry an implicit risk of further escalation. The dynamic of the interaction between governments would lead inexorably to larger and more intense nuclear exchanges. But this likelihood aside, what of the postulated 'limited' nuclear wars themselves? What would be their consequences for the civilian society unfortunate enough to live in the environs of the combatants? Because of their prominence, two possibilities must be addressed: a tactical nuclear war in Europe and an exchange between the United States and the Soviet Union against each other's missile fields.

Nuclear war in Europe

Most studies of the consequences of nuclear war in Europe have been carried out in secrecy by governments. Still, there are some public reports of the results of these analyses which can give a rough idea of what it might entail. In 1955, for example, a military exercise code-named Sage Brush was held in Louisiana. It simulated the use of 275 weapons ranging between 2 and 40 kilotons. Although detailed results were not released, it was concluded 'that the destruction was so great that no such thing as limited or purely tactical nuclear war was possible in such an area'.[12] In the same year, a second exercise code-named Carte Blanche was undertaken in Western Europe itself. In this case, the use of 335 nuclear weapons was simulated, 80 per cent on German territory. In terms of immediate German casualties alone, and so excluding the victims of radiation disease and other secondary effects, it was estimated that between 1.5 and 1.7 million died and 3.5 million more were wounded. As a result of this exercise, Helmut Schmidt stated that the use of tactical nuclear weapons 'will not defend Europe, but destroy it'.[13]

Additional war-games and exercises during the 1960s confirmed these results. They led two defence specialists to state:

> Even under the most favorable assumptions, it appeared that between 2 and 20 million Europeans would be killed, with widespread damage to the economy of the affected area and a high risk of 100 million dead if the war escalated to attacks on cities.[14]

What of contemporary weapons technology? Would the use of the weapons of the 1980s significantly alter the results of studies prepared in the 1950s and 1960s? Attempting to answer this question, the group of experts assembled by the UN Secretary General constructed a scenario for analytical purposes in which the two military alliances used a total of 1,700 nuclear weapons against each other's ground forces and nuclear arsenals in Europe. The weapons used in this war included one- and five-kiloton artillery shells and 100-kiloton bombs dropped from aircraft. It was further assumed that no weapons were targeted against cities, even though certain targets, such as armoured divisions, might well be located in densely populated areas. Although the number of weapons utilized in this analysis is large relative to the numbers assumed in the studies previously mentioned, it is still small compared to the more than 10,000 intermediate-range and battlefield nuclear weapons believed to be deployed in Europe by NATO and the Warsaw Pact.

The UN experts' group concluded that in such a situation there would be five to six million civilian casualties from the immediate effects of the explosions alone, at a minimum. (Military casualties would be about 400,000.) An additional 1.1 million civilians would fall victim to radiation disease, and countless others to the secondary effects of nuclear war. If some of the weapons were exploded on the surface, rather than in the air, as was assumed in these estimates, the number of people exposed to radiation hazards would be greatly increased. Moreover, the analysis assumed far greater control over these weapons than realistically could be expected. Some of the targets, like airbases, are located close to cities. For every one of the 200 larger weapons which went astray and hit a city, 250,000 fatalities would be added to the previously stated totals. Given the clouds and inclement weather which cover most of Europe most of the year, it is hard to believe that such accidents would not be fairly common.

It might be said that a death toll of five to six, or even ten, million, tragic as that would be, is small in comparison with the rough total of 40 million killed during the Second World War. What this argument overlooks is that the millions of fatalities that would be expected in a nuclear war in Europe would occur within a period of days, or at most weeks, and in only one region, whereas the Second World War took place over six years around the world. It also overlooks the fact that the millions of deaths projected for nuclear war in Europe are an optimistic forecast; it projects what would happen if everything went as planned. Comparable estimates at the start of the Second World War no doubt optimistically predicted a short war with relatively few casualties, as would also have been forecast at the outset of the First World War.

How realistic is the estimate of five to six million deaths in a nuclear war in Europe? Not very. It assumes fairly precise and controlled use of less than 20 per cent of the available 'theatre' nuclear arsenals. It overlooks the possibility of accidents and miscalculations. Most importantly, it ignores the ever-present danger of continuing escalation – involving either the use of additional weapons against civilian targets in Europe, or the initiation of a nuclear exchange between the territories of the United States and the Soviet Union. If millions were killed within a space of days, the difficulty of ending the conflict would be extraordinary. Emotions would devastate logic. The momentum of events would trample whatever mechanisms might be left to contain the conflict. The ultimate holocaust would almost certainly be upon us.

Nuclear wars 'limited' to strategic targets in the US and USSR
Speculations about how nuclear war between the two great nuclear powers might begin sometimes envisage one side initiating the conflict by launching a limited attack against the strategic forces of the opponent. It is expected that such an action would result from

one nation's perception that war was imminent, and its calculation that it could minimize the damage to its own society by preemptively destroying the opponent's nuclear forces. To the degree that weapons exist in each side's arsenal which would be vulnerable to a preemptive attack, such as missiles in immobile concrete silos, submarines in port, or bombers not prepared for take-off from their bases within a matter of minutes, there is a danger that such a calculation might be made in some extreme and extraordinary situation. Consequently, there has been a great deal of interest in the results of such attacks, known as 'counterforce exchanges'.

Some argue that nuclear attacks limited to opposing strategic forces would result in relatively few civilian casualties and only limited damage to industries and other civilian facilities. This raises the possibility, they maintain, that a nuclear war 'limited' to strategic forces is a feasible option. If the casualties from a counter-force attack were low, they state, the recipient would be deterred from retaliating against the opponent's civilian economy and population, for fear that if it did, the initiator would counter-retaliate, also against civilian targets, causing much greater destruction than had been incurred as a result of the initial attack.

Studies of the consequences of nuclear wars 'limited' to attacks on opposing strategic forces suggest, however, that analyses indicating that fatalities could be kept relatively low are based on unrealistic assumptions. Far more than would be the case for attacks on urban areas, the casualties from a counter-force exchange would result from radiation. Because there are many potential targets scattered throughout the US and the USSR, there is considerable uncertainty about the pattern of radioactive fall-out and its likely effects. Much would depend on the weather, the characteristics of the attack itself, and the degree to which the civilian population had taken effective steps to shelter itself from the immediate hazard of radiation. For these reasons, no official studies even attempt to estimate casualties; they concern themselves only with outright deaths. Moreover, fatality estimates depend markedly on whether attacks are assumed to be limited to opposing missile silos, or if they also are said to include bomber bases and submarine ports. The latter are typically located in or near major urban areas; attacks on them would result in much larger numbers of fatalities.

Estimates of fatalities resulting from an attack against US strategic forces range from about 2 million to about 22 million. The lower estimate assumes that the attack is restricted to missile fields and that the civilian population takes effective steps to shelter itself from radiation for a considerable period of time. Similarly, US government estimates of Soviet fatalities in the event of an attack on Soviet strategic forces, especially missile fields, range between 3.7 million and 27.7 million. Again, the crucial assumptions concern the characteristics of the attack itself and the degree to which Soviet citizens have been prepared for, and sheltered from, radioactive fall-out.

In both cases, because most strategic targets are not located near industrial concentrations, the effects on the two nations' economies would not be nearly so great as the effects of attacks directed at urban areas. Still, agriculture, livestock, and water supplies in both nations would be affected over vast areas. It is difficult to estimate the total ecological consequences, given the many uncertainties surrounding the fall-out pattern, but it seems clear that they could be profound, leading to massive shortages in grain, vegetables and supplies of meat and dairy products. Because of the smaller food stocks available to the USSR, it seems likely that the Soviet population would suffer even more than the Americans in the event of such 'limited' nuclear wars.

Even so, destruction and death on the scale envisaged in these 'counter-force exchanges' would have a profound impact on both societies. Never in man's history would such intense and widespread devastation have occurred in such a short space of time. Which society would not devolve into chaos in the wake of such destruction? Who is to say whether or not political and economic institutions would rebound from such shocks? And even if they did, the senseless deaths of millions of citizens, the physical and psychological agony of tens of millions of others, and the devastation of each nation's agricultural sector with inestimable long-term consequences would be a tragedy of unprecedented proportions.

The earth after nuclear war

'And when it is all over what will the world be like?' asked Lord Mountbatten in his famous speech at Strasbourg. 'Our fine great buildings, our homes will exist no more. The thousands of years it took to develop our civilization will have been in vain. Our works of art will be lost. Radio, television, newspapers will disappear. There will be no means of transport. There will be no hospitals. No help can be expected for the few mutilated survivors in any town to be sent from a neighbouring town – there will be no neighbouring towns left, no neighbours. There will be no help. There will be no hope.'[15]

Those who survived both the immediate and indirect consequences of nuclear explosions would face a bewildering and possibly deadly environment. Large-scale nuclear war would inject substantial quantities of nitrogen oxide into the upper atmosphere. This could erode the ozone layer in the stratosphere which protects the earth from an excess of ultra-violet radiation and lead to a significant rise in skin cancers and mutations in plants and animals. Life could be impossible in sunlight for any human being or animal not wearing special protective clothing. Scientists have suggested that damage to the ozone layer alone could have permanent and catastrophic effects on the chances that life, as we know it today, could survive on our planet.

The US National Academy of Sciences has stated that a major nuclear war could produce irreversible adverse effects on the environment and the ecological system. In ordinary language, this means that it is possible that life itself would not survive. If it did, it might not be recognizable. Radiation would cause mutations in surviving plants and animals that could change life in unpredictable ways. And the psychological trauma of the war could affect human behaviour in ways that would change human society unpredictably, to the degree that society survived at all.

Would the survivors envy the dead? Probably, if there were survivors. For this is the main question: would man, would life itself, survive? And this question no one can answer. As Jonathan Schell put it:

> In weighing the fate of the earth and, with it, our own fate,
> we stand before a mystery, and in tampering with the earth

we tamper with a mystery. We are in deep ignorance. Our ignorance should dispose us to wonder, our wonder should make us humble, our humility should inspire us to reverence and caution, and our reverence and caution should lead us to act without delay to withdraw the threat we now pose to the earth and to ourselves ... If these effects should lead to human extinction, then all the complexity will give way to the utmost simplicity – the simplicity of nothingness. We – the human race – shall cease to be.[16]

Conventional war

In this nuclear age, conventional war is too often looked at in a weaker light, as if its consequences were less dramatic and awesome. In the sense of humanity's survival, this is true. But non-nuclear wars have had devastating global effects in the past. And in a local situation, conventional warfare can have a special horror all of its own.

The Second World War was the worst tragedy the world has yet known. Nearly 40 million people were killed as a direct result of that six-year conflict: including twenty million citizens of the Soviet Union, six million Poles, four million Germans, two million Chinese. The physical devastation was tremendous – Europe and much of Eastern Asia were left in shambles.

Since the Second World War, there has been both a continuing revolution in the capabilities of conventional weapons and a consistent increase in the number of nations possessing them. Advances in the technology of modern conventional warfare have meant that military units have become more effective in their ability to destroy one another, resulting in the accumulation of larger inventories of weapons to prepare for war, and a more rapid and intense pace of interaction when war occurs. The intensity of some recent wars in the Middle East, for example, have approached the scale of the greatest battles of the Second World War. Moreover, conventional weapons have become more devastating, an unfortunate fact for the civilian populations in the path of warring armies.

The impact of conventional wars
Since 1945, there has been peace in Europe and North America, but

virtually all parts of the Third World have suffered the ravages of conventional warfare. For all practical purposes, war and internal conflicts have been so common and so brutal that casualty estimates are nearly worthless. Suffice it to note that since 1945, millions have been killed directly, tens of millions have been wounded or infected with disease, and hundreds of millions have been caught in the economic and social consequences of conventional wars.

In the past thirty years few nations in the developing world have avoided the devastation of civil or international military conflicts. In many cases, internal conflicts – wars of national aspirations or liberation, struggles between political or economic factions – have been the most brutal. Central governments frequently have turned the most inhumane weapons against their own citizens whom they believed to be sheltering dissident elements. And those contesting the government's authority have frequently resorted to terror as a means of enjoining ordinary citizens from supporting the government.

Life for the inhabitants of these afflicted regions often becomes unbearable. With their villages bombed out and devastated by government troops looking for rebel forces; their food, their possessions, and their means of livelihood appropriated by rebel groups, they often have little choice but to flee, risking the unknown perils of life in makeshift camps in foreign lands to the known horrors of conventional war in their own countries. The number of refugees from military conflicts, now temporary wards of the international community, is reaching staggering proportions. According to data gathered by the UN High Commissioner for Refugees, nearly eight million people now live in 'temporary' camps in Africa, Asia, and Latin America.

Wars themselves are ghastly enough, but in their wake, after the killing has stopped, they leave a people uprooted, traditional communal life destroyed and societies unable to cope with the economic and political whirlwind around them. Few war-torn societies escape the scourge of famine. In economic terms, the impact of famine is felt long after people again have enough to eat. The famines in Uganda and Bangladesh during the 1970s, for example, are estimated to have been the equivalent of the loss of several years' growth in those nations' gross national products. In each case, famine led to a decline in *per capita* income of 10 per cent or more. As for their social impact, that is even more devastating. It takes decades for the pulse of life to return to its normal rhythms.

The intensity of modern warfare is horrifying. During the 1973 war in the Middle East, for example, stocks of ammunition and other supplies, as well as the basic weapons of war themselves – anti-tank and air defence missiles, tanks and armoured personnel carriers, fighter aircraft – were depleted so rapidly that even though the war lasted only three weeks, both Israel and its opponents, Egypt and Syria, required emergency resupplies. Based on that experience, the major military alliances drastically revised estimates of what would be required in the event of a war in Europe.

In part, this increase in the pace of war reflects improvement in defences. Modern air defence and anti-tank systems inflict a heavy toll on offensive forces, requiring each side to employ larger numbers of weapons. The faster pace of war also reflects major advances in the rate of fire and other performance features of modern weapons, as well as the much greater logistical capabilities of the forces that support combat units.

The greater intensity of modern war means that nations tend to spend more preparing for war, both because the most modern weapons are extraordinarily expensive, and because they must maintain larger stocks in order to sustain their forces in combat. More importantly, the furious pace and intensity of modern warfare means that the pressures for escalation are greater. Increasingly, nations will not have the leisure to contemplate events, to assess the results of battle, to probe for the possibility of peaceful settlements, to attempt diplomacy. Knowing that the war cannot be sustained for long, they will feel compelled to escalate quickly, either hoping to gain the advantage of being first, or to prevent their opponents from gaining similar advantage. The implications for the scope of conventional war, should it break out among the industrialized or more militarily advanced developing nations, should be clear. Equally evident should be the implication for the danger of escalation to the use of nuclear weapons.

A second problem of modern weaponry lies in the small size and mobility of certain types of weapon. Some air defence and anti-tank missiles, for example, can be easily moved by one or two men or transported in an automobile. As these weapons are manufactured by the tens of thousands, and widely distributed throughout the world, there is a great risk of them falling in the hands of terrorists. There already have been incidents in which small bands of individuals have planned, and in a few cases actually attempted, to shoot down civilian airliners with modern air defence missiles. Unless closer controls are placed on exports and inventories of these weapons, there are likely to be more incidents in the future.

A third disturbing tendency in modern warfare is the developing use of inhumane weapons. Napalm weapons – derivatives of the First World War incendiary bombs – have been used on a major scale in virtually all major conflicts since 1945. When napalm is dropped from the air, it is a mind-chilling sight. An area not much smaller than a football pitch is smothered in a tide of orange fire. The flames leap to treetop level, burning with an immense roar everything around, billowing out a dense black smoke. A new and more lethal type of flame weapon is also now used – thickened pyrophoric agent. Within its fireball little can survive, and those within its reach are killed or wounded in a most painful way. Fuel air explosives, which destroy life by the detonation of a cloud of gaseous hydrocarbons, are a third type of weapon which, if not used for strictly military applications in unpopulated areas, have particularly inhumane results. Defoliants and other herbicides have been used extensively in Asian wars, with tragic results for those exposed and persisting effects on the local ecology. Finally, a whole range of anti-personnel weapons have been developed and are now widely deployed in the armouries of the advanced military powers. These weapons typically involve the packaging of thousands of small metal pellets within a single shell or bomb, and are designed to kill or incapacitate all people within a wide area.

War, horrible to begin with, constantly unravels new aspects of man's inhumanity to man. As so often has been the case, these weapons are frequently used not only against opposing military forces but also against civilian populations – either by accident, inadvertence, or deliberate intent. In contemporary warfare, particularly internal wars, the line between civilians and combatants is often easy to disregard. Continued international action is necessary to regulate the use of these especially inhumane weapons of war.

Chemical and biological warfare

The horrors of chemical and biological warfare appear to be peculiarly reserved for the peoples of the developing world. Except in the First World War, all confirmed and alleged cases of lethal gases or toxins being used in warfare have occurred in developing nations. Generally, the military rationales underlying these episodes appear to be (a) to neutralize forces or populations in areas too remote for infantry attack or too sheltered for air attack with conventional munitions; and (b) to demoralize through the terror of the attack either opposing forces themselves or the populations that sustain them.

The impact of chemical or biological weapons against military forces prepared for their use is questionable. The effectiveness of measures of protection against chemical attack have probably improved at a faster rate than the lethality of the weapons themselves. Modern armed forces in industrial nations, as well as the more powerful military establishments in developing nations, are equipped with respirators, protective clothing, and antidotes. Tanks and other armoured vehicles can be designed to be able to operate in chemical warfare environments, and fitted out with systems to filter and circulate purified air. As a result, when used against a prepared enemy, chemical weapons would probably only slow, not stop, military operations; forces outfitted for chemical warfare cannot move as flexibly or sustain the pace of combat as long as those who need not be concerned about gas attacks. It is this prospective ineffectiveness, far more than fear of reprisals in kind, which probably has prevented the industrial nations from utilizing chemical weapons against each other since 1919.

Chemical or biological warfare against unprepared civilian populations, however, is likely to be devastating. The suffering can be extraordinary; the deaths or associated illnesses terrifying. Some gases can be extremely lethal. A single tactical aircraft armed with nerve gas, for example, could threaten 50 per cent casualties over an area of about two square kilometres, give or take a factor of three or four depending on the weather. Indeed, this dependence of the effectiveness of chemical weapons on factors like topography and weather is probably another reason why the industrial nations have been reluctant to use them against each other. In a densely populated theatre of military operations, the only certain consequence of a chemical weapons attack is that large numbers of non-combatants would be killed. Recent computer simulations of the results of the use of nerve gas in Europe, for example, suggest that the ratio of civilian to combatant casualties could be as high as twenty to one. Should nerve gases be employed at the rate of 1,000 tons per day per side, as some military planners have anticipated, civilian casualties could be in the order of millions.[17]

Moreover, the march of technology is influencing this area of warfare as it is all others. New means of packaging chemical weapons, for example, like the so-called 'binary munitions', make them easier and less dangerous to use, and therefore more likely to be seen on the battlefield. And if research were directed at possible military applications of recent developments in the biological sciences, such as genetic engineering, the horrors that could be loosed are unthinkable.

Given the marginality of chemical and biological weapons in the security policies and military plans of the great powers, as well as the universally expressed abhorrence for such weapons, the task of outlawing them should not be insurmountable. Nevertheless, there is a stubborn resistance to their ban, particularly of chemical weapons, in the military establishments of a few countries. We on the Commission are appalled that this situation has been permitted to continue for so long. There is no excuse for the continued production, stockpiling, or use of chemical or biological weapons.

4 The economic and social consequences of military spending

Poverty, unemployment, inflation, the threat of world recession: the problems that make people and governments insecure are economic as well as military. In the 1980s, these economic problems are likely to become worse, not better, as a result of military spending.

The increase in military spending now under way threatens the economic security of all countries. The economic difficulties of the 1970s have shown that the benefits of postwar growth can no longer be taken for granted. In these circumstances, the sacrifice of human, material and technological resources required by military spending is likely to be particularly costly, for rich countries as well as for the countries which still live in poverty.

The costs of worldwide military spending are so vast that they have assumed a sort of deadening familiarity. Total military spending in 1982 will amount to over 650,000 million US dollars. This is more than the entire income of 1,500 million people living in the fifty poorest countries. The price of a single modern fighter plane would be sufficient to inoculate three million children against major childhood diseases. The price of one nuclear submarine with its missiles would provide a hundred thousand working years of nursing care for old people.

Expenditure on military goods and services is a form of consumption requiring resources that could otherwise have been used in civilian society. 'Great fleets and armies' were, for Adam Smith, writing after the English–French wars of 1756–63, the model of 'unproductive labour'. After the more lethal European wars of the 1790s, another classical economist, Jean-Baptiste Say, added the following gloss: 'Smith calls the soldier an unproductive worker; would to God this were true! for he is much more a destructive worker; not only does he fail to enrich society with any product, and consume those needed for his upkeep, but only too often he is called upon to destroy, uselessly for himself, the arduous product of others' work.'

Military consumption has increased spectacularly over time, as fleets and armies in Europe and elsewhere become more expensive and more destructive. World military expenditure is more than twelve times as great in real terms as it was fifty years ago; it is more than twenty-eight times as great as it was in 1908.

Yet such expenditure has failed in its objective of buying 'security'. The process of military spending yields decreasing returns to increasing 'inputs' of money. Even the richest military powers buy something less than security with their immense resources: military forces which may be useless in real crises; military equipment which may be matched by an enemy who emulates their military exertions. In many developing countries, the price of military 'security' is increased human misery.

Such costs seem to have become part of normal life since the Second World War. Military spending is even assumed to provide important economic benefits. One example is the 'spin-off' from military science and production for civilian purposes. Another is the 'Keynesian' benefit of increased employment. For several countries, the depression of the 1930s ended only with peacetime rearmament or war production. Could military spending also mitigate the present recession?

All these costs and benefits have been disputed throughout the history of the modern military effort. But present economic and military circumstances are likely to maximize the costs and minimise the benefits.

The present increase in military expenditure comes at a time of economic tension unprecedented in the postwar period. The 'crisis' in the world economy described by the Brandt Commission in 1980 is even more serious today. Despite rapid growth in many developing countries, the income gap between rich and poor countries is not closing. World trade declined in 1981 for the first time in over twenty years. Some developing countries do not have enough foreign exchange to buy food, agricultural inputs and investments.

The developed economies have grown far more slowly since the early 1970s than they did in the 1950s and 1960s. Productivity growth rates are lower than they were in the earlier postwar period. Unemployment is at its highest postwar level. The governments of most Western industrialized countries face large budget deficits; they must carry large public debt at high interest rates. Inflation is far higher than in the last period of widespread increases in military spending in the mid 1960s.

The military context is equally ominous. Military spending is growing rapidly in developed and developing countries and seems to be concentrated on the 'procurement' of weapons. The largest share of military budgets goes to pay soldiers and civilian government employees. Governments also buy civilian-type goods, services and structures. But it is their expenditure on specialized military equipment and research which is increasing most rapidly in the early 1980s. Buying weapons is, after all, a prime means of showing resolve in the military competitions of the postwar period.

All the major military spenders are increasing their purchases of expensive and complex conventional weapons. For most, such purchases require substantial amounts of foreign exchange to buy imported weapons. More and more developing countries import sophisticated weapons, many of which must be paid for as normal commercial transactions, rather than through military aid.

The nuclear powers are also modernizing and expanding their nuclear weapons. Nuclear forces account for less than 20 per cent of total military spending even in the countries with nuclear weapons. But their costs are concentrated on equipment: in France, for example, nuclear forces account directly for 16 per cent of the military budget, for 5 per cent of all soldiers, and for 34 per cent of the budget for military equipment.

Nuclear weapons were once justified as a cost-effective, high-productivity enterprise. There appeared to be 'no other expenditure of money for defence that will yield a greater return than atomic weapons'. The Hiroshima bomb was 'the cheapest TNT that we can make', and nuclear weapons made possible 'one worker in a laboratory substituting for fifty men in uniform'.[18] Now, after thirty years of permanent military competition, nuclear weapons are an essential part of the vast enterprise of military procurement and research.

Economic cost itself is seen as the prime index of military effort. Spending more money on defence becomes an end in itself. The

73

relative security efforts of allies and enemies are measured by the proportion of gross domestic product devoted to the military, or the absolute level of military expenditure counted in some common currency. The calculations required depend on wildly and at present unavoidably imprecise comparisons of different countries' military establishments. Military security is counted in inputs (money) rather than in outputs of 'security' or even of military goods or services. This may be inevitable in an arms race where the quality of armies is determined by metres of accuracy for missiles that have never been fired over their ultimate paths, by the potential to destroy fourteen thousand or sixteen thousand cities. But the competition to spend is likely to reduce further the economic efficiency of expenditure for military security. And it supports the false and dangerous objective of 'inflicting costs' on an enemy through an accelerated and economically debilitating arms race.

Military expenditure in developed countries

The organization of military expenditure varies greatly, so far as can be told, in different developed countries. But military expenditure is increasing in the North as a whole.[19] In the 1970s, the developed countries spent a lower proportion of their gross domestic product (GDP) on defence than in the 1950s and 1960s (although the proportion was still far higher, for most countries, than had been the case before the permanent high levels of peacetime military expenditure that followed the Second World War). This relative decline apparently came to an end in the late 1970s. The change has been most striking in the United States, where the present increase in the military share of national income follows a decline in the 1970s. Military expenditure is also increasing faster than GDP in France, the United Kingdom, Japan, and Turkey among other countries. In the Soviet Union, the military share of GDP seems to have declined slightly or remained steady in the 1970s, but may increase in coming years.[20] Military expenditure is also increasing in the German Democratic Republic (see table 4.1, p. 97).

Expenditure on military research and development is increasing even faster than overall military spending. In the 1970s, the amounts spent on military research by OECD (Organization for

74

Economic Cooperation and Development) countries grew little in real terms (see tables 4.2 and 4.3, p. 98). But here again the tendency changed in the late 1970s. The change is particularly striking in France, where military research has grown sharply since 1976, in Britain, and in the US. (In the Federal Republic of Germany and Sweden military research has declined.) There is little public information about the cost of Soviet military research. But most Western estimates suggest that military research in the Soviet Union accounts for a very large share of the military budget. With the rapid expansion in US military research proposed for 1983 to 1985, worldwide military research will continue to increase faster than military expenditure, or than national income.

In many countries, the share of pay in military spending has declined in the late 1970s – reducing the capacity of the military to generate new employment for people who are presently unemployed. This tendency seems likely to continue, at least in countries where weapons procurement is increasing rapidly.[21] Thus, official US projections show expenditures on procurement and research increasing more than three times as fast in 1981–85 as expenditures to pay military personnel. Payments to active military personnel are projected to decline from 23 per cent to 16 per cent of total military spending.

With rising military purchases, particularly of weapons and research, and continuing arms exports the production of specialized military industries is increasing.

Most military equipment is produced in a few countries – mainly the United States, the Soviet Union, France, the United Kingdom, and the Federal Republic of Germany, which together account for over 90 per cent of world military research and over 80 per cent of arms exports. Countries which import most of their major weapons use fewer skilled and scientific workers in military production, but more foreign exchange to buy military goods. In these countries the political and economic pressures associated with military spending are likely to come not so much from a 'military-industrial complex' as in arms-producing countries, but from a 'military-communal complex' – collections of local interests organized around military installations and activities in particular regions and communities.

Military spending is concentrated in a few industries which are often highly dependent on government customers.[22] It is volatile over time, changing with military needs, political circumstances, and technological innovations. Individual industries sometimes change dramatically in relative importance, as has been the case with the increase in military electronics in the 1970s.

The boom in military industries affects the environment in which decisions about military spending are made. All countries justify their military efforts on the grounds of national security. But they are all also subject – given the local and national economic impact of military spending – to pressures from the regions, industries and employees associated with the military enterprise. 'We need to recognise', wrote the American economist Arthur Burns in 1968, 'that the scale of defense expenditures has, to a significant degree, become a self-reinforcing process. Its momentum derives not only from the energy of military planners, contractors, scientists and engineers. To some degree it is abetted also by the practical interests and anxieties of ordinary citizens.' The force of this process may have been slightly reduced in the 1970s, but with the present increase in military expenditure it is likely to become even more compelling.

The effects of military spending on employment
Military expenditure, like other forms of public and private consumption, creates demand and employment. But several characteristics of the present military build-up suggest that military expenditure is not effective in reducing the kinds of unemployment that exist today.

The overall employment effects of an increase in military spending depend on the way in which the increase is financed. Military demand in OECD countries appears to create substantially fewer jobs for a given sum of money than non-military public consumption, but somewhat more jobs, at least at first, than private consumption and investment.[23] If, therefore, increased military spending were financed entirely out of increased taxes which reduced personal consumption and investment, then one could expect, all other things being equal, an initial increase in employment for a given level of national income. But to the extent that military spending substituted for investment, it would reduce economic growth and future employment.

If increased military spending were compensated for by a

76

corresponding reduction (or reduced growth) in non-military public spending – as seems to be the case in several countries in the early 1980s – then employment can be expected to fall. A detailed study of military employment in the United States estimated that a billion dollars spent on defence in 1975 would have created 76,000 jobs, compared to 80,000 for local expenditure on health, and 104,000 for local expenditure on education.[24] Since then, the contrast is likely to have become even sharper: because military purchases are concentrated in manufacturing industries while other public purchases come largely from construction and services where productivity is growing only slowly; and because pay has fallen faster as a share of military spending than as a share of other public spending.

It is possible that military expansion could be entirely financed by increased budget deficits – out of government borrowing that would not otherwise have taken place. In that case, more new employment would be created than without deficits. But such a policy seems unlikely in the early 1980s. Increased government borrowing can lead to high interest rates and thus reduce private investment. If deficits are accompanied by restrictive monetary policies, private consumption might also fall. The Western governments which are most likely to see military security as the only justification for increased public spending also seem especially determined to permit only slow growth of the money supply.

The employment created by military spending is also affected by the changing composition of spending. The trend towards a lower share of pay in military budgets is likely to reduce the employment created for a given outlay. Money spent to pay military employees generates more jobs than the same amount of money spent on other military purchases. In France, for example, one billion francs spent in 1970 to pay military and civilian personnel created 44,300 jobs, while a billion francs' worth of other military purchases created only 18,330 jobs.[25] The shift to military procurement is likely to reduce employment created – both in countries with military industries and in those which import large proportions of their purchased military goods.

The composition of military expenditure moreover determines the kind of employment created by military demand. Military expenditure in general creates jobs for skilled workers. In the

77

United States, for example, a 1968 study concluded that the defence labour force 'is generally more skilled than the civilian labour force'. At that time – when military spending was high, but less strongly biased towards technically sophisticated activities than it is now – defence employment accounted for 6.1 per cent of all workers, compared to 19 per cent of all machinists, 22 per cent of all electrical engineers, 38 per cent of all physicists, 54 per cent of all aeroplane mechanics, and 59 per cent of all aeronautical engineers.[26] Countries such as Japan which manufacture much less specialized military equipment employ fewer skilled workers in defence industries. But they too must maintain sophisticated imported equipment.

Military procurement and research require particularly highly skilled workers. The labour force in military industries is exclusive in all the main arms-producing countries. In France, for example, the proportion of engineers in 'aero-naval' industries in 1973 was five times as great as in the overall economy, the proportion of technicians over four times as great and of skilled workers almost twice as great. In the United States, over 10 per cent of employees in the aircraft, communication equipment and ordnance industries are engineers, compared to only one per cent in the overall economy. The proportions must certainly be similar in the Soviet Union and the few other countries which produce highly sophisticated military equipment.

The centrally planned economies do not suffer from unemployment in the Western sense. But they do experience social and economic costs as industrial conditions change: underemployment, human costs, costs of retraining and relocating workers. The labour force is growing only slowly in many Eastern European countries. In such countries, a rapid increase in defence procurement is likely to create disproportionate pressures on the skilled and scientific workers who are most in demand elsewhere in the economy.

One kind of military spending – soldiers' pay – does create jobs for large numbers of unskilled workers, notably young men. It thus employs workers who in most countries are relatively likely to be unemployed (although it does less for another group which has almost as high unemployment – young women). The military also employs some civilians who might otherwise be unemployed –

particularly in and around military facilities in depressed regions. But these are not the kinds of spending which are increasing fastest in the early 1980s. And the skills required both in the armed forces and for civilian military employees are presumably increasing as military equipment becomes technologically more sophisticated.

All these changes suggest that the industrial employment created by increased military spending will be of far greater advantage to engineers and technical workers – whose wages are high and whose unemployment rates are generally extremely low – than to the unskilled workers, particularly young people, who are most seriously hurt by present high levels of unemployment.

The 'Keynesian' expectation

Military spending, in sum, is not likely to return developed economies to full employment. In the 1940s, increased military spending bought boots and tanks and a mass mobilization, not research and military electronics. In the new military context, the precedent of the last depression is an illusion.

The 'Keynesian' view of military spending is in large part, of course, a political one. Its premise is that increased military spending may be the only politically plausible way of increasing public demand; that conservative governments, in particular, will only increase deficits in the interest of national security. Keynes himself, in 1940, saw economic benefits in the 'vast dissipation of resources in the production of arms': 'It is, it seems, politically impossible for a capitalist democracy to organize expenditure on the scale necessary to make the grand experiments which would prove my case – except in war conditions.' Several Marxist economists have also argued that militarism is, in Rosa Luxemburg's words, 'a preeminent means for the realization of surplus value', in part because capitalists can influence 'public opinion' in favour of military production.

Yet peacetime military spending clearly has economic costs. It creates less employment than other forms of public spending; it is highly changeable; it poses dangers for inflation. And it is no longer the only politically popular form of expenditure. The difficulty certain governments have found in cutting non-military public spending shows not only that there is continuing need for expenditure on health, welfare or old age benefits, but also that there is substantial political and public support for such expenditure. The military-industrial complex of political support for military spending is itself less unanimous than it was in the earlier postwar period – as machinists', aerospace, and metal-workers' unions in several countries have drawn attention to the economic and other costs of increased military activities.

Present economic circumstances moreover make it likely that any problems of converting resources from military to civilian use will be temporary. Eastern and Western countries have many social and other needs, which cannot be met in present conditions of slow economic growth. Projects for conversion are discussed fully in the recent and comprehensive Report of the UN Group of Governmental Experts on the Relationship between Disarmament and Development chaired by Inga Thorsson.[27]

The present level and form of military spending is not necessarily the only way in which developed countries can achieve the security they seek. Such spending, 'such dissipation of resources', should in any case only be justified on military grounds. Its economic benefits are trivial in comparison with its economic costs.

Inflation

Since the colonial wars of the 1750s or before, rapid increases in military spending have been associated with rising prices. The 'peacetime' wars since 1945 were times of inflation in Western countries. In 1950–51, the year of sharply increased weapons procurement for the Korean War, the increase in the consumer price index in the US went from less than one per cent a year to 7.9 per cent, and in Britain from 2.8 per cent to 9.7 per cent. The increase in US military expenditure for the Vietnam War in 1965–67 – and the financing of the war by government borrowing and increases in the money supply – contributed to the beginning of high levels of inflation in the US and elsewhere.

Under present conditions – in the apparently inherently inflationary world economy of the 1980s – even a much gentler increase in military spending may exacerbate inflation. Economists disagree as to the causes of inflation. Some argue that increased military spending is only likely to lead to higher prices if it is accompanied by rapid growth in the money supply. Others suggest that the macroeconomic effects of increased demand could lead to some increased inflation, even in economies with unemployed resources. Military expenditure, after all, adds to demand but unlike spending on roads, schools or hospitals it does little to improve productivity in the long term.

There are further dangers of inflation from military pressures on specific economic sectors, particularly in the main arms-producing countries. Military procurement is highly concentrated in a few industries, notably electronics. Yet the computer and electronics industries are among the few industrial sectors which are already operating at close to full capacity, thanks to strong civilian demand. Regions with electronics industries are relatively prosperous. Their engineers and technicians are close to being fully employed, and it takes several years to increase significantly the supply of such skilled people.

These are the conditions in which 'bottleneck inflation' is likely. Build-ups which look small compared to the entire economy can look large relative to the output of the industries where the demand actually takes place. The military sector must attract workers and equipment from civilian industries by offering to pay higher prices or wages. Sudden large increases in demand cannot be met and must be rationed off with price increases for military output and also for civilian goods produced by the same industries.

The process of military procurement is itself inherently inflationary. Military purchasing involves risky and volatile demand, the need for high-quality output and markets with a single buyer, few sellers, and little foreign competition. These circumstances seem to be peculiarly conducive to price increases, at least in market economies with large military industries. Thus in the United States, in 1972–80, the implicit price deflator for 'national defence purchases of electronic equipment' increased by 6.6 per cent a year, while the deflator for 'personal consumption expenditures for radio and television receivers' increased by only 1.6 per cent a year. Studies for Britain, the Federal Republic of Germany, Sweden and France show similar discrepancies between military and consumer prices in the 1960s and early 1970s.[28]

The overall consequences of such inflationary processes are impossible to predict. They are likely to be most significant in arms-producing countries which increase their military spending rapidly. It is worth noting, none the less, that in the largest such Western country, the US, official analysts do anticipate 'bottleneck' problems. The 1982 Report of President Reagan's Council of Economic Advisors comments that defence expenditure 'will be concentrated in the durables sector', and 'will add to pressure on the durables manufacturing sector'. In real terms, according to the report, weapons procurement and research and development 'will grow at an estimated rate of 16 percent annually between 1981 and 1987. This exceeds the 14 percent annual rate of increase that occurred during the 3 peak years of the Vietnam buildup.' The 'anticipated' effects may be higher 'relative prices in at least some of the affected industries', 'delays in the delivery of military goods', and 'some temporary crowding out of private investment'.[29]

Arms-importing developed countries and countries where military spending increases only slowly are generally less subject to inflationary pressures from increases in military spending. But they must, of course, use increasing amounts of foreign exchange if the price of the arms they import increases, as is likely to happen if bottlenecks occur in major arms-producing countries. And the experience of the period since 1965 suggests that inflation in one country – particularly ones as important in trade as the US and the other main military spenders – is transmitted very rapidly throughout the world economy.

Eastern European economies will not be immune to the effects of such generalized inflationary pressures. They may also, if their own military purchases increase rapidly, experience scarcities, delays or rationing. As in market economies, specialized military equipment is produced in concentrated industries, by highly skilled workers. In the Soviet Union, military industries appear to be more isolated from civilian production than in market economies – yet the planning process itself may make adjustment to bottlenecks particularly difficult.

Economic growth and economic structure
In the longer term, the costs of military spending are likely to be even higher. The peculiar character of the present military expansion – its uneven demand for technical workers and for the output of mechanical and electronic industries – poses particular problems in the conditions of the post-1973 economic crisis.

Military security requires the sacrifice of other forms of private and public consumption. It can also, by reducing investment, lead to the sacrifice of future consumption, of economic growth. The determinants of economic growth are complex and idiosyncratic. Yet even a cursory examination of different countries' performance suggests that those countries whose military spending has been relatively high over the postwar period – the US, the Soviet Union, the UK – were not best equipped to withstand the economic troubles of the 1970s. Many of the large and small economies where growth remained high – Japan, Canada, Finland, Austria, Hungary – spent relatively little on the military.

In OECD countries, military expenditure has been shown to have had a negative effect on investment. Military spending was in the 1950s and 1960s a substitute for investment in future productive capacity and in civilian public structures.[30] This may have happened because monetary policies and interest rates reduced funds available for private investment; military demand for mechanical equipment may have increased the cost of capital goods purchased from the same industries. The consequences of such forgone opportunities are likely to be particularly serious under present conditions of slow economic growth.

Military spending seems also to have reduced investment in Eastern Europe. The government of Czechoslovakia has said that disarmament would increase 'productive capital investment' and thereby help to meet 'unsatisfied' capital requirements – under particularly favourable conditions 'since to a large extent the productive capacities involved [in the military] are in the sphere of engineering'. In the Soviet Union, too, military activities are likely to have reduced investment. Some Western economists have estimated that an increase in Soviet defence spending in the 1960s would have involved 'a decline in new capital investment by almost the full amount of the increase in military outlays, and a retardation of output growth that peaked several years after the initial shock'. More recent studies suggest that the effects would be particularly serious to the extent that the increase were concentrated in procurement and military construction.[31]

Military demand may further reduce economic growth by limiting technical change in the civilian economy. In countries with military industries, military demand is of disproportionately great importance in the goods-producing and above all in the 'metal products'

83

sectors of the economy.[32] These industries are the main loci of technical change – the employers of the greatest concentration of scientists and technicians, the sectors that perform most industrial research, the source of essential capital goods and industrial inputs.

Technical change is generally assumed to have been a major source of economic growth and productivity growth in the postwar period. It is needed most urgently in the 1980s: to generate new employment, to create new industries and to increase productivity in the growing public and private service sectors. Yet if the military build-up continues, the technological potential of the main arms-producing countries may be increasingly influenced by military demand. This would pose special problems for countries where employment and output is growing most rapidly in the services sectors – where increasing military production could thus consume a growing share of a diminishing industrial sector and reduce competitiveness in industrial exports.

The sacrifice of technical possibilities is equally serious for other major powers – for the Soviet Union, for example, where an advanced military sector coexists with a civilian economy in which output per person is well below the average for developed countries. The volatility of military demand may also pose particular problems for centrally planned economies, in ways that could further reduce the possibilities for growth. As a Soviet expert wrote in a paper for the Commission, military crises 'require that pre-set priorities be changed, make it necessary to look for additional resources, hinder normal performance of a centrally planned economic mechanism'.

Military science and technology

Research and development (R&D) have been an essential component of military power since the mobilization of scientists during the Second World War. R&D account for over 10 per cent of total military spending in the US, France, and the UK; their share is at least as large in the Soviet Union.

The sums devoted to military research far exceed those for any other public research objective. Defence accounts for half of all publicly financed research in Britain and the US, and more than a third in France. In West Germany, by contrast, it accounts for only 10 per cent, and in Japan 2 per cent. Britain alone spends more public money on defence R&D than all the OECD countries together spend on research for environmental protection, transport, and telecommunications. The US spends more on defence R&D than all OECD countries' publicly financed research on energy production, industrial growth, and agriculture, and more than the entire public research expenditures of West Germany and Japan together.

Such a commitment of resources requires economic and social sacrifice. The supply of scientific labour and equipment is limited, at least in the medium term. Resources used for defence are not available for purposes of civilian innovation, economic growth, social or medical progress. The sacrifice required is particularly costly to the extent that the resources in question are of high quality – the nation's 'strongest scientific collectives', in the phrase used by Leonid Brezhnev of Soviet defence scientists and designers.

The 'spin-off' from military science could compensate to some extent for these lost opportunities. Military research and innovation can have subsequent civilian applications or spin-off: from standardized parts developed under the pressure of nineteenth-century war to advances in nuclear energy, aircraft and electronics stimulated by the permanent scientific mobilization since 1945. In the long term, military demand can increase the supply of scientists, engineers, and their equipment.

But such spin-off benefits can never fully match the costs of military research. Civilian research presumably has greater total benefits for the civilian economy than does military research. Increased military research can only make the civilian economy better off if there is little possibility of increasing civilian research. Arguments about spin-off thus depend on a political premise analogous to that implied in 'Keynesian' expectations about military employment, and equally unprovable; that resources used in military research have, as a matter of political reality, no alternative use – they would not otherwise be used for directly civilian purposes. As in the case of military spending and employment, military research should only be justified on grounds of security: its economic costs will always be greater than its economic benefits.

Specific applications of military technologies – of which the most spectacular are to be found in parts of the electronics industry – have provided major benefits to particular industries. But military

85

spin-off may be of less civilian use in the 1980s and 1990s than it was in the earlier postwar period.

The objectives of the nuclear powers in the present military build-up look particularly unpromising. It is impossible to predict the quirks and delays by which scientific discoveries are translated into subsequent technologies. But industrial countries urgently need technological innovations to reduce costs of production and limit inflation, to create new employment, to improve health and reduce the costs of medical care. Such social objectives are not obviously congruent with the pressing military priorities of the Soviet Union and the United States – from silent nuclear submarines to guidance for intercontinental ballistic missiles, and communications systems for the period following a nuclear war.

It is possible, too, that military involvement may alter the character of a country's scientific institutions, even when it provides extra resources for scientific work. Military science requires qualities – secrecy and the isolation of scientists – which are not necessarily favourable to civilian research, or to the civilian diffusion of discoveries. The most spectacular applications of American research in military electronics have come not in the US but in a country – Japan – with a different and impeccably civilian organization of science, technology, and commercial innovation; whose military industry is about the size of its toy industry; and which, with an economy over half the size of that of the US, spends less than one hundredth as much public money on military research.

Countries which spend heavily on military research – notably the United States and the United Kingdom – have a large scientific base, as measured by the proportion of GDP dedicated to research and development. But the civilian research effort of these countries has grown less rapidly than that of other large OECD countries, and is now smaller relative to GDP than in several other countries. From 1967 to 1979, total civilian R&D in the US, the UK, and France remained constant or declined as a share of GDP, while in West Germany and Japan they increased by almost 50 per cent.[33]

In centrally planned economies, where military research institutes are often isolated from design bureaux and from military industries as well as from civil production, there are also limitations on spin-offs. The effects of military secrecy may reduce the quality

86

of military and non-military research.[34] Soviet leaders have indeed urged increased spin-off in machine building; as Leonid Brezhnev has said, 'taking into account the high scientific-technical level of defence industry, the transmission of its experience, inventions and discoveries to all spheres of our economy acquired the highest importance'.

Military R&D may, finally, have consequences which go even beyond their opportunity costs, more or less imperfectly mitigated by subsequent economic benefits. The perpetual motion of military science may be one of the most important forces sustaining present high levels of military expenditure and military insecurity.

Many scientists and soldiers – Mountbatten and Admiral Rickover, government science advisers such as Kistiakowsky, Wiesner, and Zuckerman – have testified to the momentum of military science. As Zuckerman has written:

> ideas for a new weapon system derive in the first place, not from the military, but from different groups of scientists and technologists who are concerned to replace or improve old weapons systems ... At base, the momentum of the arms race is undoubtedly fuelled by the technicians in governmental laboratories and in the industries which produce the armaments.

The destabilizing effects of military R&D are even more serious to the extent that research is committed to the search for a qualitative breakthrough, an ultimate weapon. One cannot look at the history of the nuclear arms race, of bombs and missiles invented and deployed, without doubting whether competition in military research has added to the security of any nation.

Military expenditure in developing countries

The costs of military competition are qualitatively different in developing and developed countries. In both the South and the North, the military uses government revenues which could otherwise be spent on health or on education, on improving people's lives. In both it uses scarce technical and industrial resources. But in many developing countries, these sacrifices increase human deprivation. Even in high-income developing countries, military spending can jeopardize economic growth and development, and thus the foundation for lasting security.

The character of recent military expansion makes these costs especially great. Developing countries' purchases of sophisticated, mostly imported weapons have increased dramatically since the early 1970s. And a large share of their weapons imports are not part of military aid programmes as in the earlier postwar period, but commercial purchases which must be paid for with foreign exchange. The economic costs of military spending are likely to increase in the 1980s; any economic benefits will be small.

Trends in military expenditure

Statistics on military activities in the Third World are of even poorer quality than for industrialized countries. But the past decade has clearly been one of great expansion, both in the quantity of weapons, and in their sophistication.

The cumulative military expenditure of the developing countries amounted to US $316 thousand million in 1975-79, measured in 1978 prices. $147 billion was by OPEC countries and $169 billion by other developing countries.

Over the 1970s reported military expenditure in developing countries, including China, rose by 6 per cent a year in real terms, compared to only one per cent a year in developed countries. The developing countries' share of world military expenditure increased from 19 per cent in 1971 to 25 per cent in 1980. The pattern of expenditure, of course, varies enormously by region. China's military spending is far larger than that of any other developing country, and is estimated to be about one third as great as military spending in the US and the Soviet Union; it appears, however, to be constant in real terms, or slightly declining.[35] In the Middle East, where spending is rising fastest, *per capita* military expenditure is greater than in Europe; in South Asia, total military expenditure for almost one billion people is less than the military budget of Italy alone.

The overall increase in military spending was fastest in the mid 1970s. But the early 1980s appear to have brought a new acceleration. Rich and poor countries have participated in the military build-up. In the oil-exporting countries with surplus capital (Saudi Arabia, Iraq, Libya, and the smaller Gulf oil exporters) military expenditure increased more than sixfold in real terms in the 1970s, and Saudi Arabia has surpassed Britain as the sixth largest military spender. Yet the capital surplus countries still accounted for only one third of all military spending by developing countries. Oil-importing developing countries doubled their military spending in real terms in the 1970s, as did the poorer oil-exporting countries.

Arms imports increased even more rapidly than overall military spending. Cumulative arms imports by developing countries were worth $65.2 billion in 1975–79 in constant 1978 prices, $32.3 billion worth by OPEC countries, and $32.9 billion worth by other developing countries.[36] Developing countries imported $5.6 billion worth of weapons in 1970 (measured in constant 1978 US dollars) and $16.1 billion worth in 1979. All categories of countries participated in the expansion. In 1977–79, the capital-surplus countries accounted for less than a third of developing countries' arms imports. In those years, six oil-importing developing countries – including two with *per capita* incomes below $200 in 1979 – imported more than a billion dollars' worth of arms. The composition of military spending has thus shifted, as it is shifting in developed countries, towards the procurement and maintenance of armaments, and away from paying armies.[37]

Arms production in developing countries has also increased substantially in the 1970s. Brazil and India have well-established arms industries. Other newly industrializing countries, including Taiwan, Singapore, and South Korea, have expanded their military production. Their output ranges from sophisticated military aircraft produced under licence or indigenously designed to ammunition and cheap electronic equipment. Brazil exports military aircraft to at least nine developed and developing countries, and several other developing countries have increased their export of new or secondhand military goods.

The economic consequences of arms imports
Developing countries' arms imports are worth twice as much in absolute terms as the arms imports of all developed countries. The discrepancy in relative terms is far greater. Thus, two poor countries, Ethiopia and Somalia, spent more on arms imports in 1977–79 than did all the Nordic countries plus the Netherlands. Arms imports were worth less than 0.1 per cent of the national

income of the six European countries, but about 14 per cent of the national income of the two African countries. Their cost was equivalent to the income of 36,000 people in the European countries, but of 5,000,000 people in the African countries.

Until the 1970s, a large proportion of developing countries' arms imports were paid for by the exporting countries as part of their military aid. Now, much of the cost of far more complicated and expensive arms is paid by developing countries themselves. Although capital-surplus countries have increased their own military aid, this relieves little of the burden of arms imports for most countries.

Arms imports thus require foreign exchange, either earned or borrowed, which could otherwise be used to buy investment goods (or which in the short term might buy food and agricultural inputs such as fertilizer). Some part of the money spent on weapons would undoubtedly not be available for other purchases, notably loans by arms-exporting countries which would not be forthcoming to finance civilian goods. Even these loans, however, must eventually be repaid. And foreign exchange spent to buy arms, unlike that spent on investment goods, does not increase a country's capacity to earn foreign exchange in the future and thus to pay interest on and repay existing debts.

Almost all developing countries now face declining prices for their exports, and many must make debt service payments at high interest rates. In these circumstances, the burden of paying for arms imports becomes even more likely to reduce economic growth. For several countries, the value of arms imports is large relative to their total deficit. The low-income oil-importing countries' arms imports were actually worth more in 1977–79 than their cumulative current account deficit. In Africa, arms imports were equivalent to 8 per cent of the total value of imports in 1977–79, compared to less than 2 per cent in 1970. Unless they somehow match these foreign exchange outlays with an export push, some African nations may be forced in the 1980s along the path of a country such as Peru, which contracted large commercial bank loans in the mid 1970s, many of which were used to finance arms imports. When credit was later cut back, Peru was obliged to follow highly deflationary economic policies in a stabilization programme arranged with the International Monetary Fund.

Arms imports – however they are financed, and once the weapons have actually been delivered – also require skilled labour for their operation and maintenance. Scarce technical and managerial workers who would otherwise contribute to civilian capital formation are preoccupied with military undertakings. The country's ability to 'absorb' civilian projects is strained, and it gets less growth from its existing investment. Some arms imports undoubtedly contribute to economic growth. Countries in the Middle East for example import 'military construction services' as well as military hardware, acquiring roads and ports that can be used for civilian as well as military purposes; and foreign military technicians can presumably impart civilian skills during their tours of duty. But these effects are likely to offer only small compensation for the overall costs of military imports.

Economic growth and economic structure
Military spending reduces economic growth in developing countries. The most recent econometric findings (for sixty-nine countries in the 1950s and 1960s) show that increases in military spending had significant negative effects on rates of growth. They also show that increased military spending reduced both investment and agricultural production. On average across countries, a one-per-cent increase in the military share of GDP was associated with a 0.23-per-cent reduction in the investment share of GDP, and a 0.18-per-cent reduction in the share of agriculture.[38]

These findings suggest that, as in developed countries, military spending in developing countries uses resources which would otherwise be available for domestic investment. The effect is likely to have been even greater in the 1970s, to the extent that military spending was increasing fast and shifting towards procurement of sophisticated imported equipment. The negative effects on agriculture suggested in the econometric studies could also have adverse social and economic consequences. If military spending leads to a reduction in food production, the outcome could be increasing dependence on food imports and reductions in the real incomes of the poorest people, in both the cities and the countryside.

In many countries, including the poorest arms-importing countries in Africa, even the 'civilian-type' goods and services which are produced locally in developed countries must be imported: such countries import uniforms and army boots, and even construction materials and technicians for building simple military facilities. There is little possibility that military production will stimulate economic growth in these countries.

The ways in which military spending affects economic growth and structure vary enormously in different countries. Military spending is more likely to stimulate growth in developing countries with military industries. Yet these industries have flourished in countries which already had a diversified manufacturing industry.

There are other countries, including several which are now 'newly industrialized', which benefited economically from the postwar arms race between the great powers. Taiwan, South Korea, and Greece received large amounts of US military and economic aid in the 1950s and 1960s. Such aid helped ease foreign exchange bottlenecks, while overall demand was kept high by domestic military spending. But like any other single factor, the military effort can explain only a part of these countries' economic history. They had other opportunities, of which they took advantage. By contrast, ties to great powers and ample foreign aid did not transform Turkey, Iran, and Egypt into prosperous new industrial economies. And other fast-growing countries, such as Brazil, the Ivory Coast, and Mexico, were far more removed from the direct effects of the wars and cold wars which have occurred since 1945.

Can military spending none the less have positive 'Keynesian' effects in developing countries, even those without military industries? Unemployment and underemployment are after all endemic in virtually all the poorer developing countries. Much of the increased demand for military equipment flows to suppliers abroad. But construction workers on military bases and newly employed soldiers and sailors – Adam Smith's 'unproductive' workers – spend their wages, and this spending could give other people jobs.

There are several reasons to doubt that increases in overall demand coming from the military will stimulate output and growth in most of the Third World. Total production in a developing economy is likely to be strictly limited, though the constraining forces differ from time to time. They all centre on shortages of scarce inputs into the production process – land, physical capital, foreign exchange, or skilled labour. With output held down by scarce resources, an increased share devoted to the military can only come about through reductions in other forms of demand such as civilian consumption purchases or capital formation.[39]

Even the direct employment benefits of the defence effort may be small. As in developed countries, military spending creates jobs for people who already have them. The military employs skilled people, often in and around large cities and ports; the people who are underemployed tend to be unskilled workers, and people living in the countryside. The exact fit, or misfit, of military demand and economic structure depends, of course, on the particular sort of military security that a country wants. One can easily imagine armies whose organization and equipment and geographical dispersion are such as to create large numbers of jobs for unemployed people: armies which are used for development and employment.

But present tendencies – a military effort organized around sophisticated and imported equipment – do not seem to favour such benefits. The trade in aircraft and missiles and ships is also a trade in ideas – ideas about military strength, about the organization of military expenditure.

Certain effects of military expansion can also impede economic and social development more generally. There are dangers for any country that adopts 'alien lifestyles and ideologies', and a 'military culture'. Just as armies could be used to reduce underemployment, so they could also encourage useable skills, complementary military and civilian projects, indigenous social development. But these alternative ideas of security are hardly dominant in the military boom of the 1970s and early 1980s. As in developed countries, military spending should be justified as a way to buy 'security', not for its economic benefits.

The arms trade in the world economy

The import and export of weapons have become an essential feature of international trade in the last ten years. This commerce is likely to have serious economic costs for arms-importing developing countries. It has evident benefits for exporting countries. But in the long term it may not be in the economic self-interest of either group, or of the world economy as a whole.

The arms export boom was one of the ways in which certain

market and non-market developed economies adjusted to the financial changes of the 1970s. Through arms exports, they shifted part of their increased oil costs to developing countries, including oil-exporting countries.

Since the first oil price increase of 1973, the 'capital surplus oil exporters' have shared a trade surplus which increased from $3 billion in 1972 to $40 billion in 1975 and $85 billion in 1980, measured in 1978 prices. The developed countries as a whole adjusted relatively rapidly to the first oil shock. The industrial market economies shifted to deficit after 1973 but regained a surplus by 1975; the centrally planned economies excluding China had a $9 billion deficit in 1975, but reached a trade balance by 1978. The overall deficit, in sum, fell most heavily on the oil-importing and non-surplus oil-exporting developing countries. These countries' deficit increased from $18 billion to $53 billion in 1975, and $43 billion in 1978.

Arms sales played a significant role in this triangular process of adjustment, at least for the few countries which account for almost all arms exports. The estimated value of developed countries' net arms exports to the rest of the world increased from $6.3 billion in 1970 (measured in 1978 prices) to over $16 billion a year in 1977–79, including $13 billion a year from the United States and Soviet Union. This was equivalent to over half of the developed countries' total current account surplus.

Arms exports assumed a financial importance in the process of 'recycling' oil revenues which exceeded their overall economic weight. In 1977–79 the developed countries' arms exports to the rest of the world amounted to less than 2 per cent of their total exports. Developing countries' arms imports were worth less than, for example, remittances from these countries' emigrant workers. Yet the rapid increase in the arms trade magnified its consequences. In the 'resolution' of the second oil shock of 1979, arms exports may play a comparable role. Once again, the non-surplus developing countries face a sharply increased deficit. Once again, arms sales to developing countries appear to be increasing substantially in the early 1980s as they did in 1974–75.

But conditions in the world economy are in several respects even more dangerous than they were in the mid 1970s. The developing countries were then able to increase their imports of arms and other goods from developed countries – because their own export earnings increased, because of greater foreign aid from developed and oil-exporting countries, and because many of the middle- and higher-income developing countries contracted large commercial loans. This process of adjustment avoided financial crises, and also helped to maintain economic growth in both developing and developed countries.

Such adjustment seems less likely in 1982. The prices of primary commodities exported by developing countries have declined sharply, and their exports of manufactured goods are threatened by recession and protectionist pressures. Developed and oil-exporting countries – their own finances squeezed by slower growth and increased domestic public spending, including military spending – seem unwilling to increase substantially their foreign aid. Continuing high interest rates have reduced the commercial borrowing of many developing countries, and increased the burden of existing debt. In 1981, even before the full effects of high interest rates became felt, the total volume of world trade actually fell for the first time since the 1950s.

The foreign exchange burden of arms imports is even greater under these circumstances than it was in the mid 1970s. The longer-term costs are correspondingly more serious – in reduced investment, reduced prospects for future export earnings, and worsened insecurity in the world economy.

The costs of military spending

Military spending is a charge on the economic future of all countries, the richest and the poorest, those who import and those who export arms, the East and the West. Its economic consequences are in certain respects similar in the most diverse countries. Everywhere, it demands resources which are already scarce and which are becoming yet more scarce in the early 1980s.

The economic benefits of military spending are trivial in comparison with its economic costs. Military expansion will not stimulate full employment as it did in the 1940s. If it competes for scarce government finances with social expenditures it is likely, instead, to reduce employment. It carries the risk of worsened inflation. Many of the jobs it creates – in all the countries which buy

95

or sell sophisticated weapons – are for scarce scientific or skilled workers.

A military expansion – above all one that is concentrated in the procurement of advanced weapons and military research – is also likely to reduce future economic growth. In developed and developing countries, both centrally planned and with market economies, military spending appears to reduce investment in productive capacity, or in facilities such as hospitals and schools. It imposes a heavy burden on Eastern economies whose labour force is growing only slowly. Military research and training can provide incidental or spin-off benefits for civil society, but these are less than would be achieved from direct investment in civilian research. Many countries, too, have some form of dual economic structure in which a modern industrial sector coexists with a less productive agricultural sector (in developing countries) or with a growing sector providing social and other 'unproductive' services. In such countries, a sophisticated military effort makes disproportionately great demands on the modern industrial sector, causing further structural difficulties.

The importance of such costs varies immensely from country to country. There are some eighteen countries who consistently spend less than 1.5 per cent of their national income on the military. These countries avoid most direct military costs.[40] Yet no country is free from the economic consequences of worldwide military spending. For the waste and distortion of human effort involved in modern military competition threatens the security of countries collectively as well as individually.

The principle of common security which underlies this Report asserts that countries can only find security in cooperation and not at each other's expense. This principle applies to economic as well as to military security. Countries are joined together by economic interdependence as well as by the threat of destruction. All countries are hurt if military spending reduces the economic well-being of major participants in the world economy. All are hurt if military demands on government finances limit aid or commercial lending to developing countries. Economic recovery requires a common effort to increase trade. Without economic recovery there is no hope for common security – for the common prosperity which is the basis of security itself.

Table 4.1 Military expenditure as a percentage of gross domestic product: selected developed countries.

	1950	1960	1970	1976	1977	1978	1979	1980	1981
Australia	3.0	2.7	3.5	2.9	2.9	2.8	2.7	2.8	—
Belgium	—	3.6	2.9	3.1	3.1	3.3	3.3	3.3	3.3
Canada	2.6	4.2	2.4	1.8	1.9	2.0	1.8	1.8	1.8
Czechoslovakia	—	4.0	3.9	3.1	3.1	3.1	3.1	3.2	—
FR Germany	4.4	4.0	3.3	3.5	3.3	3.3	3.3	3.3	3.4
France	5.5	6.5	4.2	3.8	3.9	4.0	4.0	4.1	4.2
German DR	—	1.2	4.5	4.1	4.0	4.1	4.2	4.4	—
Greece	6.0	4.9	4.8	6.9	7.0	6.7	6.3	5.6	5.9
Israel	4.7	5.5	23.8	27.2	25.5	20.9	20.2	(14.0)	—
Italy	4.3	3.3	2.7	2.3	2.4	2.4	2.4	2.4	2.5
Japan	—	1.1	0.8	0.9	0.9	0.9	1.0	—	—
Netherlands	4.8	4.1	3.5	3.2	3.5	3.2	3.4	3.3	3.4
Poland	—	3.5	4.0	2.6	2.7	2.6	2.7	2.8	—
S. Africa	0.8	0.8	2.0	4.1	4.6	4.2	3.8	3.2	—
Spain	—	2.2	1.6	1.8	1.7	1.7	1.7	—	—
Sweden	3.5	4.0	3.6	3.2	3.3	3.3	3.3	3.1	—
Switzerland	2.6	2.5	2.2	2.3	2.1	2.1	2.2	2.1	—
Turkey	6.2	5.1	4.3	6.2	5.8	5.2	4.3	4.3	4.8
UK	6.6	6.5	4.8	4.9	4.8	4.6	4.7	5.1	5.0
USA	5.1	9.0	8.0	5.4	5.3	5.1	5.2	5.6	5.8
USSR	—	(12.4)	(12.0)	(9.9)	(9.5)	(9.2)	(9.1)	—	—
Yugoslavia	—	7.2	5.0	5.6	5.3	4.9	4.6	—	—

Source: *SIPRI Yearbook* 1980, 1982. Figures given for countries with annual military expenditure of over $2,000,000,000 in 1981 (in 1979 US $). Figures in parentheses are SIPRI estimates. Official Soviet estimates are shown in note 20 on p. 199.

Table 4.2 Public research and development expenditure on defence, selected OECD countries (in thousands of millions of US dollars at 1975 prices and exchange rates)

	1971	1975	1979	1980	1981
United States	10.4	9.7	10.4	10.4	11.5
United Kingdom	1.1	1.4	1.6	1.7	1.6
France	—	1.2	1.5	1.6	—
West Germany	0.6	0.6	0.6	0.6	—
Sweden	—	0.2	0.2	0.1	0.1
Japan	—	0.1	—	—	—
Canada	—	0.1	0.1	—	—
Italy	0.03	0.02	0.03	0.03	—
Switzerland	0.04	0.03	—	—	—
Netherlands	0.04	0.03	0.03	0.03	0.03

Source: OECD, *Science and Technology Indicators*, July 1981.

Table 4.3 Public expenditure on defence research and development as a percentage of GDP, selected OECD countries

	1971	1975	1979	1980	1981
United States	0.73	0.60	0.61	0.59	0.64
United Kingdom	0.52	0.61	0.66	0.59	0.57
France	0.33	0.35	0.39	0.41	—
West Germany	0.16	0.14	0.13	0.12	—
Sweden	—	0.24	0.20	0.18	0.18
Japan	—	0.01	0.01	—	—
Canada	0.06	0.03	0.03	—	—
Italy	0.02	0.01	0.01	0.01	—
Switzerland	0.07	0.05	—	—	—
Netherlands	0.05	0.03	0.03	0.03	0.03

Source: OECD, *Technical Change and Economic Policy* (1980), p. 40; OECD, *Science and Technology Indicators,* July 1981.

Table 4.4 Military expenditure as a percentage of gross domestic product, selected developing countries

	1950	1960	1970	1976	1977	1978	1979	1980
Argentina	2.8	2.3	1.9	2.2	2.0	2.3	2.5	2.0
Egypt	—	(5.8)	16.2	24.9	22.5	(13.3)	(9.6)	—
India	—	1.9	3.0	3.2	3.0	2.9	2.8	—
Indonesia	—	5.4	3.1	(4.9)	4.3	4.2	3.6	2.3
Iran	—	4.3	6.6	12.4	10.9	—	—	—
Iraq	—	7.1	11.2	11.2	10.4	—	—	—
Korea, S.	—	6.1	3.8	5.8	5.9	6.2	5.4	6.0
Kuwait	—	—	3.9	6.6	7.5	7.1	(5.0)	—
Libya	—	—	(4.1)	(8.3)	(7.5)	(11.7)	—	—
Malaysia	—	2.2	4.1	4.4	4.7	4.6	4.1	5.6
Nigeria	—	0.5	5.8	4.4	4.5	4.0	—	—
Oman	—	—	11.6	32.8	26.9	29.6	22.9	22.3
Pakistan	—	2.8	6.1	5.5	5.4	5.3	5.0	5.2
Saudi Arabia	—	—	(11.8)	(14.4)	(14.8)	(16.3)	(16.5)	—
Syria	—	—	11.9	14.8	15.3	14.0	21.1	16.6
Taiwan	—	10.5	8.5	7.5	(8.3)	(8.5)	—	—
Thailand	1.6	2.6	3.2	3.5	3.3	3.3	3.6	3.4

Source: *SIPRI Yearbook*, 1980, 1982. Figures in parentheses are SIPRI estimates. Figures given for developing countries whose annual military expenditure in 1980 exceeded $1,300,000,000 (in 1979 US $), and for which figures are available. SIPRI does not publish estimates of Chinese military expenditure as a percentage of GDP.

5 A positive approach to security

The costs and dangers of the arms race – the acceleration of political tension and instability, the persistence of conventional military conflicts, the rising danger of nuclear war, the growing economic and social burdens of military spending – will not be eased if the nations of the world persist in pursuing security along familiar avenues. So long as they insist on trying to protect national interests unilaterally, behaving as if their security can be gained at the expense of others, they will fail. The well-worn path of military competition is a blind alley; it cannot lead to peace and security.

In the opening pages of this report we outlined an alternative approach to security. It is our firm conviction that adoption of these principles would lead to a better world, a world in which all people could lead richer and more complete lives, free from the fear of war and the threat of annihilation. Toward these ends, we urge all nations to rethink their security policies. We hope that political leaders and ordinary people throughout the world will come to recognize, as we have, that security can be achieved only in common, in cooperation with one another. We urge further that the principles outlined in Chapter 1 form the basis for the security policies of all nations, and that states act in common to build security on this basis.

In practical terms, application of the principles of common security must be tailored to the realities of political and military circumstances in specific situations. The close relationship between progress towards political accommodation and prospects for arms negotiations has been one of the guiding principles of our approach to security issues; little can be accomplished if these ties are not recognized. Few specific means of limiting arms and moving towards disarmament have universal relevance; fewer still are feasible at a given moment in all parts of the world. It is best, therefore, to pursue a 'building-block' approach towards limiting arms and achieving true security. It is possible to move towards a variety of different measures simultaneously, but most must be tailored to the special conditions in different parts of the world or specific aspects of particular military problems. As such initial measures are achieved, a broader political momentum may develop, making possible the consideration of increasingly ambitious steps.

In effect, the agenda of negotiations and agreements set out in Chapter 6 of this report constitutes the first phase of a programme for disarmament. It has been constructed piece by piece as a result of our analyses of specific problems concerning particular types of military force in specific regional settings.

Thus, in order to set the stage for our recommendations, it is necessary to review the current situations in several politico-military contexts. We concentrate on situations that raise the greatest common dangers of conventional or nuclear war and excessive expenditure on armaments. Our purpose is to identify the salient factors that must be taken into account in designing solutions to these security problems, and to define the opportunities, scope, and specific directions that negotiated solutions might take most advantageously.

Curbing the nuclear arms race between the US and USSR

The distribution of power and wealth is inequitable in international society. The same is true of military capabilities. Advanced technologies and great financial resources are necessary to develop and field large, modern armies; thus restricting the number of states which engage in such activities on a major scale. The two major nuclear powers account for more than 95 per cent of all the nuclear weapons in existence. Together, they account for the largest share of the world's military expenditure. Respectively, the two lead the world's most powerful military alliances – NATO and the Warsaw Pact. Politically and diplomatically, more than any other nations, these two influence developments throughout the world.

It is therefore essential that the United States and the Soviet Union play active roles in promoting worldwide progress towards arms limitation and disarmament. Real progress could not be accomplished without their cooperation. The realization of common security would prove extremely difficult without the endorsement and participation of both major nuclear powers.

The most dangerous aspect of US–Soviet competition concerns nuclear weapons. The nuclear arsenals of the two powers are so large that if they were ever used the destruction would be unprecedented, threatening the continuance of life on this planet. Moreover, both are expanding their nuclear stockpiles. According to official American estimates, the number of nuclear bombs and warheads deployed in the Soviet and US strategic offensive forces will reach 8,000 and 9,400, respectively, in 1982. At the same time, both US and Soviet nuclear weapons and delivery systems are becoming increasingly more accurate and destructive, particularly in their ability to threaten the other side's nuclear forces.

These increases in the size of the two forces and advances in their capabilities are taking place within the confines of the 1972 SALT Interim Agreement on Offensive Arms and the 1979 SALT II Treaty. Although the latter has not yet been ratified and the former expired five years ago, both signatories have continued to abide by their terms. If these restrictions were no longer observed, the strategic arms competition could accelerate rapidly.

Overall, the 1979 treaty confines the two sides to no more than 2,400 land-based and sea-based missile launchers and heavy bombers. Once ratified, the treaty would cause this aggregate ceiling to be lowered to 2,250. Moreover, the provisions of the treaty place important restrictions on the composition of the two sides' forces and, to some extent, limit the opportunities for modernization of existing weapon systems. To understand the impact of these constraints, and thus their potential importance, it is necessary to examine the structure of the two sides' forces in some detail.

About two thirds of the Soviet Union's strategic offensive capabilities are concentrated in land-based intercontinental ballistic missiles (ICBMs). In June 1979, when the SALT II Treaty was signed, there were 1,398 operational ICBM missile launchers in the Soviet inventory. These included older missiles, known in the West as SS-9s, SS-11s, and SS-13s, some of which have since been retired, as well as newer RS-16, RS-18, and RS-20 ICBMs, each of which is equipped with multiple independently targetable reentry

102

vehicles (MIRVs). Under the terms of SALT II, the Soviet Union may deploy no more than 820 ICBMs with multiple warheads, and the number of warheads with which each missile may be equipped also is restricted. These ICBMs with multiple warheads are the Soviet strategic weapons which cause the greatest concern in the West as – technically at least – they could be capable of destroying American ICBMs in a counter-force strike. According to Soviet spokesmen these multiple warheads constitute a response to the US MIRV programme and do not indicate a counter-force strategy.

The Soviet Union also maintains a large and modern force of strategic submarines with ballistic missiles. In June 1979, there were 950 such missiles on 62 submarines. The Soviet Union also is introducing newer types of submarine and submarine-launched missile, the latter with multiple warheads. RSM-50 missiles are already operational, while a still more capable missile, known in the West as the SS-NX-20, is expected to be deployed soon on the new Typhoon-class submarine. Assuming that they deployed the maximum number of land-based missiles with multiple warheads permitted by SALT II, the treaty would restrict the Soviet sea-based force to no more than 380 missiles with MIRVs. Finally, in June 1979 the Soviet Union maintained a force of 156 heavy bombers.

The Soviet Union has signed the 1972 Treaty on the Limitation of Anti-Ballistic Missile Systems and adhered to its terms for more than ten years. The Soviet Union – like the United States – is reported to maintain a programme of research in ballistic missile defence technologies. Unlike the United States, the Soviet Union has not dismantled the one operational anti-ballistic missile site which it is permitted by the treaty. According to Soviet spokesmen, this is explained by the fact that the Soviet Union confronts nuclear powers in addition to the United States. The Soviet Union also has an extensive air defence system, including thousands of surface-to-air missile launchers, interceptor aircraft, and radar. This system is continuously being modernized. According to Soviet spokesmen, both factors are due to the strength of the American air force and the Soviet Union's geopolitical situation. Finally, the USSR also devotes attention to civil defences and to anti-submarine warfare forces.

103

More than one half of the US strategic warheads are deployed as submarine-launched ballistic missiles. In June 1979, there were 656 such missiles on 41 submarines. These included Polaris A-3 missiles with single warheads, Poseidon C-3 MIRVed missiles, and Trident C-4 missiles with multiple warheads, which are now entering the force on new Ohio-class submarines and to replace older missiles. So long as the provisions of SALT II remain in effect, the United States, like the USSR, can deploy a total of no more than 1,200 MIRVed sea-based and land-based missiles. The US is also developing a new submarine-launched ballistic missile, the Trident D-5, which could be operational after 1990, and would be more capable than existing missiles.

The United States also deploys a large force of B-52 and FB-111 strategic bombers. In June 1979, there were 574, about 220 of which were in storage. The SALT II Treaty prohibits the US, like the Soviet Union, from deploying more than a total of 1,320 ballistic missiles with multiple warheads and bombers equipped with cruise missiles, and also limits the average number of cruise missiles with which each bomber can be equipped. Cruise missiles are singled out by the Soviet Union, among other weapons, as greatly complicating the negotiation and verification of arms control agreements. According to US spokesmen, the cruise missile programme is necessitated by improvements in Soviet air defences.

Also in June 1979, the United States had deployed 1,054 land-based strategic missiles. One thousand of these were Minuteman ICBMs, of which 550 were equipped with multiple warheads; the others were 54 Titan missiles with single, but more destructive warheads which are now being dismantled. The United States is developing a new and powerful type of land-based missile, the M-X, which could be operational in 1986. These new missiles would be capable technically of destroying Soviet ICBMs in a counter-force strike. According to American spokesmen, the M-X is necessary to offset similar Soviet capabilities.

The United States has signed the 1972 Treaty on the Limitation of Anti-Ballistic Missile Systems and has adhered to its terms for more than ten years. The United States – like the USSR – pursues research in ballistic missile defence technologies and has stepped up these programmes somewhat in the past few years. The US also maintains anti-submarine warfare forces and a research programme in these technologies. The large US air defence system built during the late 1950s was dismantled, for all practical purposes, ten years later. Recently, the US administration has called for a reinvigoration of strategic air defence and civil defence, but these plans were not approved by the US Congress in the spring of 1982.

As they are modernized and augmented, both sides' strategic forces are acquiring characteristics which seem to suggest the possibility that they might one day be used to fight nuclear wars. As the strategic postures evolve in this direction, the situation becomes more unstable and dangerous than when the sole purpose of strategic forces seemed to be to deter the outbreak of nuclear conflict. Improvements in the accuracy of missiles, advances in command and control and targeting systems, and the proliferation of weapons increasingly convey the impression that the two sides see a potential role for strategic forces in combat.

We on the Commission are firmly of the mind that there would be virtually no likelihood of limiting a nuclear war, once begun, and consequently no possibility of 'victory' in any meaningful sense. Were the United States and the Soviet Union ever to cross the nuclear threshold, all nations would be involved in a process whose course would lead to unprecedented destruction. The very process of destruction would render prior calculations and attempts to exercise control practically, impossible. Any doctrine which postulates the possibility of waging nuclear war victoriously thus risks the most dangerous gamble that humanity has ever taken.

We believe that doctrines which postulate fighting limited nuclear wars are dangerous. They create the illusion of control and thus might tempt political leaders in untoward situations 'to risk all in one cosmic throw of the dice'. And they lead to the deployment of weapons and other systems which create incentives for one side or the other, if it became convinced that war was likely, to strike first, hoping in vain to limit the devastation it would suffer in retaliation. In short, limited nuclear war doctrines and strategies lead to a high risk that, one day, nuclear war actually might begin.

Aside from its implications for the risk of nuclear war, the nuclear arms race has adverse consequences for the development of better political relations between the great powers. The interactions between the arms race and political relations are complex, of course. But it is clear that significant progress in one could not continue indefinitely without progress in the other.

Nor are the political implications of the US–Soviet nuclear arms competition restricted to their relations with one another. Everyone, the world over, would suffer in the event of a US–Soviet nuclear war. And the existence of their nuclear arsenals plays a role in each of the great power's relations with other nations. Just as the destructive potential inherent in their nuclear arsenals poses an implicit threat to the security of mankind, so too does the existence of these forces affect the nature of the relationship that each is able to maintain with both allies and non-aligned states. The ties between North and South and relations within the two major military alliances would change for the better if the US–Soviet nuclear arms competition were successfully restrained.

Neither the US nor the USSR accepts responsibility for the strategic arms race. The two nations must move together to contain the strategic competition, implementing the principles of common security so as to stabilize the balance between them, and to reduce substantially the size of forces on both sides and to limit qualitative improvements.

The Commission places great importance on measures to rekindle progress in US–Soviet nuclear arms talks. As a first step, it would be desirable to ensure that the accomplishments of the past – particularly the 1972 Treaty on the Limitation of Anti-Ballistic Missile Systems and the 1972 Interim Agreement on Strategic Offensive Arms, as well as the 1979 SALT II Treaty – continue to be observed. Beyond this, it would be desirable to reopen bilateral US–Soviet negotiations about strategic offensive forces and make rapid progress. To avoid a failure of this process, both sides must exercise great restraint in the deployment of new weapon systems.

It also is essential that the other nuclear weapon states – Britain, France, and China – eventually join in arrangements to contain nuclear arsenals. It would be unrealistic to expect the US and USSR to move very far towards nuclear disarmament if other nations continue to develop and expand their own nuclear capabilities. It is reasonable to expect the two major nuclear powers to take the first steps. But they will have to be joined by the other nuclear weapon states, if the stability of an effective arms control regime is to be preserved and additional progress made towards disarmament.

The process of strategic arms talks is indispensable; it affects the very climate and framework of international relations. It is essential therefore that the US and USSR move immediately to reaffirm the limitations and restraints that the SALT II Treaty provides, to agree on any necessary clarifications or adjustments of the treaty in that connection, and to seek a follow-up treaty providing for sharp reductions and qualitative limitations resulting in essential parity at substantially lower and more stable levels of forces.

Security in Europe

The major military confrontation between East and West takes place in Europe. Here we find the greatest concentrations of conventional and nuclear military power anywhere in the world. Both alliances allocate relatively large shares of their total national resources to the armed forces. Because both sides understand the stakes to be great, in the event of crisis the risk of war could be high. Moreover, the arms they believe are necessary in Europe to maintain their security are a major factor driving the continuing build-up of US and Soviet military power.

Recognizing this problem, some countries in Europe have decided to remain neutral, outside military alliances, and to alleviate in that way the intensity of political and military confrontation on the continent.

The danger of war in Europe today seems less acute than it did only twenty years ago, when the armed forces of NATO and the Warsaw Pact confronted one another in a most dangerous crisis. Still, if trends towards the deterioration of political relations between East and West and towards increasing deployments of military forces on both sides continue, intense crises could once more dominate our lives. If war did come to Europe, the consequences would be devastating and extend far beyond the continent.

The military confrontation in Europe is a powerful obstacle to political cooperation and *détente*. Competition and concern for military security dominate the outlook. The experience of the 1970s indicate that political *détente* will wither away unless it is sustained and followed up by agreements for the limitation and reduction of arms. The maintenance of large armies in Europe increases the difficulty of achieving viable political balance and durable, cooperative relations. The large deployments of nuclear forces aggravate these problems and raise special risks of their own.

Changes cannot occur overnight. But a process must be set in motion. The military confrontation in Europe not only reflects but also exacerbates basic political differences. It has developed its own momentum. As new quantities and qualities of weapons appear, suspicions mount and reactions multiply. Pressures for additional spending on military forces thus grow. The risk of war is heightened.

Conventional forces
The balance of conventional forces in Europe is difficult to assess. A multitude of factors like geography, military organization, doctrine, and possible contingencies complicate the picture. Geography affords advantages and disadvantages to both alliances. The Warsaw Pact has greater tactical depth and the potential to reinforce its units on the frontlines rapidly. But the USSR's access to the seas is restricted. While the members of NATO can mobilize and reinforce defensive positions rapidly, the area of Western Europe is relatively shallow and major reinforcements must cross the Atlantic Ocean (see discussion p. 24).

One basic measure of military strength is the size and mobilization potential of ground forces. Differences between the two sides' force structures complicate such assessments, however. Problems of comparison and measurement have troubled the negotiations in Vienna on mutual troop reductions in Central Europe. The talks have taken place since 1972 without resulting in agreement.

Central Europe is the core area of the military confrontation in Europe. It is the most sensitive politically. The two sides' figures for the manpower each presently deploys in Central Europe, the potential area of reductions if agreement could be reached in Vienna, have proven difficult to reconcile. There is a difference of some 150,000 men between the Eastern and Western estimates of

Eastern manpower. No procedures have been found for resolving this so-called 'data issue'.

Nevertheless, considerable progress has been made in the talks. The parties are in accord that an agreement should result in collective equal ceilings of 900,000 men in the area of reductions, with a subceiling of 700,000 men in ground forces. In addition, special subceilings would apply to Soviet and American troops. Reductions would take place in two phases. The first would include withdrawal only of Soviet and American troops from Central Europe. In the second phase, the forces of other countries participating directly in the talks would be included in the reductions. The parties have not yet agreed, however, on the linkage between the two phases of reductions, including the rules governing the distribution of reductions among states participating in the second phase.

The parties also have agreed that the implementation of reductions should be accompanied by associated measures designed to stabilize the agreement by facilitating verification and promoting confidence. The two sides have not agreed, however, on the scope and content of such measures, nor on whether associated measures should apply to some extent beyond the area where troop reductions would occur. Finally, the parties are in accord that an agreement on reductions should contain guarantees that the security of states outside the reduction area in Europe would not be diminished.

The remaining differences in the negotiations on mutual force reductions in Vienna are not large enough to justify prolonged stalemate. Failure to reach agreement soon would hamper progress towards increased cooperation, greater security, and mutual confidence in Europe. It could prevent agreements on the limitation and reduction of nuclear weapons in Europe. There is an urgent need to break the stalemate.

Battlefield and intermediate- (medium-) range nuclear weapons
The pernicious consequences of continued military confrontation are multiplied by the presence of large numbers of nuclear weapons of many types on the continent of Europe. In the event that any nuclear weapons were used in a conflict in Europe, there would be a

great danger of rapid and widening escalation. There is an urgent need to consider ways of reducing the number of nuclear weapons in Europe and constraining the role which they play in the defence planning of the two alliances.

The rationale for deploying nuclear forces in and around Europe has changed over time. NATO states that so-called 'theatre' nuclear forces serve the function of deterring large-scale conventional attack, compensating for the perceived inferiority in its conventional forces, also deterring first use of nuclear weapons by the other side, and providing a link to American strategic nuclear forces. Comparable considerations seem to influence force planning in the Warsaw Pact.

The Soviet Union and Warsaw Pact countries have offered to renounce the first use of nuclear weapons, but the NATO countries have not felt able to respond positively, explaining this by the threat of a large-scale Warsaw Pact conventional attack. No proposal has been advanced combining a 'no-first-use' pledge with a negotiated agreement on approximate parity in conventional forces at agreed levels.[41]

Against this background, the Commission has concentrated on steps to reduce the chance of the early use of nuclear weapons, to give greater confidence in the conventional force balance, and to raise the threshold for making any decisions that could lead to the use of nuclear weapons.

Today NATO has deployed some 6,000 nuclear warheads in Europe. The Warsaw Pact inventory is of a similar magnitude. These weapons fall into several categories. According to the Soviet view: *medium-range weapons* are those with a range (action radius) of 1,000 kilometres or more, but less than intercontinental range (action radius), which is usually taken as 5,500 kilometres; *tactical (and operational) nuclear weapons* are those with a range of less than 1,000 kilometres. According to Western classifications, there are *short-range weapons* (0–150 kilometres), *medium-range weapons* (150–1,500 kilometres), and *intermediate-range weapons* (more than 1,500 kilometres) in Europe.

Short-range or tactical systems are sometimes referred to as battlefield weapons. They include artillery and short-range missiles capable of firing either conventional or nuclear munitions. A large portion of the nuclear munitions in Europe are intended for battlefield weapon systems.

Medium-range weapons, as defined by the West, include missiles and aircraft. NATO operates 180 medium-range Pershing IA missiles in Europe, 108 with US forces and 72 with those of the Federal Republic of Germany under a two-key system. All of the American missiles of this type are scheduled to be replaced by intermediate-range Pershing II ballistic missiles. According to Western sources, the Warsaw Pact also fields medium-range missiles and is developing a successor with greater range, the SS-X-23. Still longer-range Soviet SS-12 missiles are also being replaced by SS-22 missiles. Also according to Western sources, the total number of Warsaw Pact medium-range missiles is between 600 and 700, all of which are deployed on Soviet territory.

Both sides also deploy a large number of dual-capable aircraft in Europe. It is not known how many of these actually are assigned to nuclear missions. All told, perhaps one third of the nuclear munitions in Europe are assigned to systems of the medium-range category. NATO's 'theatre' nuclear munitions are stored in special sites in peacetime. Similar Warsaw Pact sites are found in Eastern Europe.

France also maintains medium-range nuclear weapons. It presently has 42 launchers for the Pluton short-range missile, but these eventually will be replaced by the 200–300-kilometre range Hades missile. In addition, France operates 30 Mirage IIIE and 40 Jaguar dual-capable aircraft, as well as two aircraft carriers each with a squadron of 24 dual-capable Super Etendard aircraft.

Some weapons fall outside these categories. They include atomic demolition munitions (nuclear mines) and air defence systems. NATO has announced it is reducing its reliance on nuclear air defences; its new air defence missile, Patriot, will have only a conventional capability.

Battlefield nuclear weapons, as well as nuclear air defence systems and atomic demolition munitions, raise important problems of stability. Air defence systems would likely create pressures for delegation of authority to use them before combat actually was initiated. Battlefield weapons also would create pressures for early use in any armed conflict. Their location near the front lines of any war would mean that political leaders may face a choice early in a conflict of either authorizing the use of battlefield weapons or watching them be overrun. Each side's fears that the other side might resort to 'first use' could intensify crises and multiply the dangers of the initiation of nuclear conflict and its escalation.

Both parties may perceive battlefield weapons as links in a chain of deterrence from conventional to strategic nuclear warfare, made necessary by the existence of similar weapons on the other side. Security for both sides would improve if these weapons were mutually reduced and withdrawn. These weapons are currently not the subject of East–West negotiations. They should be, and urgently.

Dual-capable aircraft represent a factor of ambiguity as they bridge the division between nuclear and conventional weapons. A clearly distinguishable threshold is an important prerequisite for stability in crises. Airfields and aircraft are vulnerable to attack and may invite preemptive strikes early in a crisis or war. Such pressures are multiplied by arrangements for so-called 'quick reaction alert', in which aircraft or missiles are loaded with nuclear munitions and maintained ready for instant launching. Such arrangements could lead to escalatory pressures for the early use of nuclear weapons. Consideration should be given to the possibility of discontinuing the practice of maintaining such forces on nuclear alert. The existence of nuclear air defence systems also could stimulate pressure for the early use of nuclear weapons and the pre-delegation of authority to fire them. Their continued deployment should be seriously reconsidered.

The distinction between nuclear warfare and conventional operations also could be eroded through the introduction of either so-called 'mini-nukes' or enhanced radiation ('neutron') weapons. Proponents of both types of weapon emphasize their war-fighting advantages, thus suggesting the dangerous chimera of limited nuclear war as a matter of deliberate policy.

The military postures of both alliances in Europe thus presently incorporate and rely heavily on large numbers of nuclear weapons of different ranges. This constitutes not only a threat to the stability of East–West relations, but to the very survival of humanity. These facts have caused and are likely to continue to generate increasing popular opposition. There is a need for both sides to reorient defence priorities and reduce dependence on nuclear weapons. In our view, the concept of common security provides a basis for

112

viable arrangements which, unlike the present postures, would not generate unsettling tensions between East and West, and between citizens and their governments.

Intermediate- (medium-) range nuclear forces

The issue of intermediate- (medium-) range nuclear forces has generated considerable controversy in recent years.

In the late 1950s, NATO deployed intermediate- (medium-) range ballistic missiles of the Jupiter and Thor types in the United Kingdom, Italy, and Turkey, while long-range Matador cruise missiles, subsequently replaced by Mace-B, both capable of reaching the Soviet homeland, were deployed to Western Germany. All these weapons were withdrawn in the early 1960s. In December 1979, however, NATO made its two track decision to deploy 108 Pershing-II ballistic missiles and 464 long-range cruise missiles, all with single warheads, in Europe. The United States also operates about 250 intermediate- (medium-) range aircraft, known as F-111s, many of which are deployed in Europe.

The Soviet Union has deployed intermediate- (medium-) range missiles against targets in Europe since the mid to late 1950s. According to Western data, by the mid 1960s, some 750 SS-3, SS-4, and SS-5 ballistic missiles had been deployed in the USSR. The deployment of a new mobile intermediate- (medium-) range ballistic missile equipped with three nuclear warheads was initiated in 1977. Some 300 of these SS-20 missiles, with a total of 900 warheads, the major portion of which can reach targets in Europe, are reported by the West to be operational. All SS-3 missiles have been retired. SS-4 and SS-5 missiles also have been retired as the SS-20s have been deployed, but many of them remain operational. In addition, the Soviet inventory of intermediate- (medium-) range forces includes some 400 aircraft, many of which are older models, and some of which operate from bases in Asia.

Britain and France also operate intermediate- (medium-) range nuclear forces. The British force currently includes Polaris submarine-launched ballistic missiles and Vulcan bombers. The latter are being phased out. The former are scheduled to be replaced by Trident D-5 missiles with a total of about 520 warheads.

France maintains a force of 18 SS-2/3 intermediate- (medium-) range land-based ballistic missiles with single warheads plus five submarines with 80 M-20 missiles with single warheads. The latter will be replaced by M-4 missiles, each with six warheads. Two more French submarines are planned, resulting eventually in a force carrying 672 warheads. France also operates about 30 Mirage-IV medium bombers.

It is hard to calculate the balance of intermediate- (medium-) range nuclear-capable systems. In the Soviet view, there is rough parity in delivery vehicles between the two sides, about 1,000 each. The Western position is that the balance favours the Warsaw Pact overwhelmingly.

The French and British claim their forces are of a different nature than US and Soviet intermediate- (medium-) range forces, in view of their strategic deterrent functions. The British and French forces so far have not been included in SALT, but they clearly influence assessments of the East–West balance.

Some intermediate- (medium-) range systems raise other problems because their locations suggest that they would be capable of attacking targets either in Asia or in Europe. Intermediate- (medium-) range systems overlap also with shorter-range systems, particularly dual-capable aircraft. From the point of view of the Soviet Union, several types of aircraft constitute an integral part of the American strategic threat to its homeland. From the Western perspective, these aircraft serve tactical purposes and, in any event, could be vulnerable to preemptive, disarming attack. Similar systems on the Soviet side threaten targets in Western Europe. From the point of view of Western Europe, the deployment of intermediate- (medium-) range nuclear weapons raises issues concerning the political balance in Europe. From the Soviet perspective, such concerns are overdrawn and insincere. Such problems of perspective and calculation indicate the need for an integrated approach to negotiations.

The Soviet Union and the United States have initiated negotiations in Geneva on the limitation and reduction of intermediate- (medium-) range nuclear weapons capable of reaching targets in Europe. These negotiations were the consequence of a continuing debate between NATO and the Warsaw Pact in 1979–81 concerning intermediate- (medium-) range weapons. The debate covered the ratification of SALT II, the SS-20 programme of the Soviet Union, the NATO decision to deploy new

intermediate- (medium-) range weapons, conditions for negotiations between the US and the Soviet Union, and proposals for
moratoria on deploying such weapons.

The NATO decision of December 1979 had a double character. It
was a decision (a) to produce and deploy new intermediate-
(medium-) range weapons, and (b) to negotiate mutual limitations
with the Soviet Union. NATO is seeking a sharp reduction in Soviet
intermediate- (medium-) range weapons leading to abstention from
the deployment of its new weapons.

The preceding analysis suggests the importance of also
resuming negotiations on the reduction and limitation of strategic
offensive forces, since the two kinds of weapon overlap in
important ways. Parallel negotiations would enable the parties to
view limitations and reductions in the context of an overall balance.

Furthermore, the negotiations on intermediate- (medium-) range
nuclear weapons should be thought of as the first step in a process
that eventually would include all nuclear weapons capable of
reaching targets in Europe. Some land-based weapons of shorter
range, when based forward, are capable of reaching the same
targets in Europe as intermediate- (medium-) range systems.
Consequently, at a minimum, collateral constraints would be
needed to prevent circumvention of an agreement limiting
intermediate- (medium-) range systems. Negotiated limits on and
reductions of these shorter-range weapon systems would be an
alternative way of solving this problem. It is important that during
such talks both sides avoid measures that could undermine the
negotiations.

The overall objective of negotiations should be approximate
parity at the lowest level of forces, taking into account the overall
relationship of military forces. The negotiated levels should be low
enough that NATO would forgo the introduction of a new
generation of intermediate- (medium-) range nuclear missiles in
Europe.

Chemical weapons
Today, chemical weapons are of relatively secondary importance in
the arsenals of the two alliances. However, there are disturbing
signs which may herald changes for the longer term if preventive
action is not undertaken. Expanded production of nerve gases,

115

development of so-called binary munitions, as well as the awesome possibility of exploiting recent advances in the life sciences for military purposes – all underline the urgent need to ban chemical weapons altogether.

Most of the arsenals of chemical weapons are kept on the national territories of the United States and the Soviet Union. Estimates of stockpiles are extremely uncertain, but depots are reported to exist in Central Europe. It also is uncertain whether chemical weapons are distributed to troops in the field, but it is unlikely that they are because of their toxic nature and resultant need for special safety precautions.

An agreement on the destruction and ban of chemical weapon stocks in Europe would be an important step towards the universal abolition of chemical weapons. It would reconfirm the presumption against the use of chemical weapons which was laid down in the 1925 Geneva Protocol.

The use of chemical weapons would cause large-scale collateral damage, particularly to the unprotected civilian population. Effective protective clothing may be issued to troops, however, and such equipment also may provide protection against radiation from nuclear explosions. Hence a ban on training troops with chemical weapon protective clothing, combined with an agreement on the withdrawal of chemical weapons from Europe, would probably be more acceptable if it were also combined with arrangements for the withdrawal of battlefield nuclear weapons. The problem of chemical weapon attacks from outside the proscribed area, against forces in that area, also would have to be dealt with by collateral constraints.

Cooperation and confidence building

Security in Europe is not only a matter of the limitation and reduction of arms. It is a function of the quality and scope of international relations in Europe. Cooperation in commerce, cultural affairs, the exchange of people and ideas, in meeting the challenges of industrial society, and in promoting a more equitable international economic order are important fields of endeavour which will shape the future political order in Europe.

The 1975 Helsinki Conference on Security and Cooperation in Europe (CSCE) adopted a Final Act which incorporates the notion

116

that security can be strengthened by cooperative measures to build confidence in the peaceful intentions of all sides, as well as by attention to humanitarian issues and the principles of international conduct.

The confidence-building measures in the Final Act also include a commitment to announce twenty-one days in advance military manoeuvres which involve the participation of more than 25,000 troops. States whose territory extends beyond Europe are obliged to announce manoeuvres which take place in an area extending 250 kilometres from the border with other European states. States may, if they choose, invite observers to be present at smaller military manoeuvres, and states may also give prior notification of major military movements.

During the Helsinki Conference follow-up meeting held in Madrid during 1981 and 1982, participating states agreed in principle to convene a Conference on Disarmament and Confidence and Security Building Measures in Europe. The first phase of such a conference would be devoted to a consideration of a 'new generation' of confidence- and security-building measures which should apply to the whole of Europe. Following the conclusion of at least a first-phase agreement on mutual force reductions in Vienna, negotiations about more substantial reductions in military forces could take place in a second phase of the Conference on Disarmament and Confidence and Security Building Measures in Europe.

There are essentially two kinds of confidence-building measures which are relevant to the situation in Europe: those which inhibit the use of military activity to exert political pressures, and those which reduce the danger of surprise attack. The confidence building measures included in the Helsinki Final Act were of the former kind. Measures negotiated in the future should have stronger elements of the latter. The specific measures to be discussed should relate to information, notification, observation, and stabilization. They should probably concentrate on overt military activities such as manoeuvres, troop movements, and deployments of weapons and troops that may be used for surprise attacks. The approach should strive to develop standards for routine military activity through agreed guidelines for reporting, observing, and limiting the size and scope of such activities. They may in the future extend also to such areas as budgeting, planning, and research and development, possibly through cooperation in a specially created consultative commission.

Curbing qualitative aspects of armament competitions

The development of modern armaments, whether nuclear, chemical or conventional, is based on extensive military research and development. Both the US and USSR allocate substantial resources to the pursuit of new military technologies in amounts which constitute a serious burden on available scientific and technical talent and research facilities. These high levels of military research are unprecedented in peacetime. Several other industrial nations, and a few developing states, also have organized military research and development efforts.

New military applications of advanced technologies can sometimes be useful in stabilizing the balance between rival nations – for example, new methods of verifying arms control agreements and more effective command and control systems. More often, however, new military technologies lead to new instabilities. Even though most results of military research and development are not particularly revolutionary, their emergence on one side creates pressure for the other major power to develop similar capabilities and also to strive itself even more forcefully to regain the qualitative lead.

Fear of technological inferiority causes nations to expand their military scientific establishments, thereby strengthening bureaucratic and corporate interests which favour a continuance of the arms race. There is also the familiar cycle of arms and insecurity. The technological competition contributes to doubts and suspicions on each side and, eventually, to the deterioration of political relations; this in turn leads to greater pressures for the development of new weapons. In other words, the race for technological sophistication and qualitative advantage becomes self-perpetuating. The drive for newer and better weapons also contributes in a significant way to the rising cost of military equipment, further compounding the adverse social and economic

118

effects of the diversion of scientific and technical resources from social needs.

For all these reasons, efforts should be made to curb the momentum of qualitative aspects of arms competitions. This can not be done by mere declarations, however. There is a need to negotiate concrete controls on specific military technologies.

To some extent, restricting qualitative aspects of arms competitions must be the responsibility of each nation individually. The internal dynamics of technological research can probably never be matched by negotiated agreements alone. Negotiations have repeatedly been outpaced by technology. Scientists and other citizens, military officials, and political authorities in all nations must come to understand that not all advances in military technology contribute to greater security; that many – perhaps most – actually lead to dangerous instabilities and a greater risk of war. Thus, when designing new weapon systems, national authorities should take care that such weapons would not make it excessively difficult to negotiate verifiable arms control agreements. Similarly, weapons which would raise the incentive to initiate nuclear war also should be avoided.

Restricting military research and development through negotiations is difficult. Improvements in the capabilities of weapons typically result from a multiplicity of technological advances in various individual components. For example, improvements in the accuracy of missiles result from purer rocket fuels, advances in computers incorporated in missile guidance systems, more detailed and accurate maps of potential targets, better understanding of the earth's magnetic field, and advances in the ballistic design of the reentry vehicle, to mention only some. Improvements in the accuracy of ballistic missiles raise troubling implications for the ability of retaliatory forces to survive a first strike, and thus for the stability of the nuclear balance. This danger has led many to suggest that measures should be taken mutually by the US and USSR to negotiate restrictions on missile accuracy. But compliance with negotiated prohibitions of advances such as those just described would be very difficult to verify.

This means that constraints on qualitative advances in weapons must focus on stages in the development process at which advances in military technology become more visible; this is the point at which developments in various components of a weapon system are put together into a complete prototype and tested. It already has been demonstrated that nations can successfully negotiate agreements that limit the testing and subsequent deployment of weapon systems. The 1963 Limited Test Ban Treaty, for example, and the 1974 Threshold Test Ban both placed restrictions on the testing of nuclear weapons. Similarly, restrictions on the development of certain types of anti-ballistic missile systems have been defined by the signatories of the 1972 treaty to come into effect at the point that such developments would be assembled as prototypes and tested in the field; so too have restrictions on missile developments contained in the SALT II Treaty. In considering, therefore, how to restrict qualitative aspects of the armaments competition it may be best to concentrate not only on those aspects which raise the greatest concern for the stability of military relations among nations, but also to focus on restrictions on the testing and deployment of new types of weapon.

In our view, the following types of limitation might be the most important for initial efforts to control the qualitative competition in armaments.*

A comprehensive ban on nuclear testing and nuclear proliferation

According to the Stockholm International Peace Research Institute, there were nearly 1,300 nuclear explosions carried out between 1945 and 1980; by now, the total probably exceeds 1,500. These data are summarized in table 5.1, p. 122.

Efforts to end nuclear tests have resulted in the 1963 Limited Test Ban Treaty that banned nuclear tests in the atmosphere, under water, and in outer space. More than 100 nations have now ratified or acceded to the agreement. Neither China nor France, of the nuclear powers, however, have yet acceded to the convention. And, of the so-called threshold countries, the nations which are believed

---

* In the view of Giorgi Arbatov, the Soviet proposal to prohibit the development and manufacture of new types of weapon of mass destruction may also be an important step to limit dangerous aspects of the qualitative arms race.

to be in a position to develop nuclear weapons fairly rapidly, both Argentina and Pakistan have signed, but not yet ratified the treaty.

Also, in 1974, the United States and the Soviet Union signed a treaty limiting the permissible yield of nuclear tests. This was followed in 1976 by a second bilateral treaty limiting the yield of nuclear explosions for peaceful purposes. Neither of these agreements has yet been ratified, however.

In any case, all three of these agreements are a far cry from a comprehensive ban on nuclear testing. Such a treaty is the key element in any programme to limit the spread of nuclear weapons and to reduce the threat of nuclear war.

Technically speaking, a complete ban on the testing of nuclear weapons would make it difficult for most nations to develop an operational capability to build or use nuclear weapons. At the least, it would mean that any nation which developed nuclear weapons surreptitiously could have only limited confidence that they would work as planned. This would lead states to be even more reluctant to explode a device than they might be if they had been able to test it. Moreover, a ban on nuclear testing could retard the development of the weapons of the present nuclear powers, making it more difficult for them to develop nuclear bombs and warheads of new designs or based on new physical principles.

A comprehensive nuclear test ban would be even more important politically. It would demonstrate that the nuclear powers had taken seriously the pledge they made in the 1968 Non-proliferation Treaty to move towards nuclear disarmament. Fulfilment of this promise is essential if, over the long term, the non-nuclear powers are to be expected to continue to abide by their pledges to forgo acquiring nuclear weapons. A comprehensive test ban would be a crucial step towards a world in which nuclear weapons played a less prominent and less dangerous role. A comprehensive ban on nuclear tests also would enhance the acceptability and credibility of the Non-Proliferation Treaty, which works to limit the spread of nuclear weapons.

Once there was a comprehensive ban on nuclear tests, it would be easier to strengthen the system of safeguards and controls to discourage nuclear proliferation. The International Atomic Energy Agency, based in Vienna, has done considerable work in this regard, but it is evident that even more progress would be desirable.

121

Table 5.1 Number of nuclear explosions

Time period	USA	USSR	France	UK	China	India	Total
1945–50	8	1	0	0	0	0	9
1951–56	72	50	0	9	0	0	131
1957–62	202	113	6	14	0	0	335
1963–68	190	58	24	2	8	0	282
1969–74	111	101	28	1	8	1	250
1975–80	84	124	39	7	10	0	264
Total	667	447	97	33	26	1	1,271

Source: Stockholm International Peace Research Institute: *World Armaments and Disarmament, 1981* (Taylor and Francis, 1981).

Particularly important might be further safeguards against the diversion to weapon programmes of fuels used by non-military nuclear reactors.

Limitation of military activities in space

The United States, the Soviet Union, and several other nations make use of space for military purposes. For the most part, these activities are of a nature which contributes to a more stable military balance and a lower risk of war. Military satellites are used to provide warning of missile launches, for example, as well as for rapid and reliable communications between political authorities and military commanders. These activities as a rule contribute positively to a more stable nuclear balance by reducing fears of surprise attack and the dangers of unauthorized or inadvertent release of nuclear forces. The Commission is concerned, however, about the possibility of more dangerous military activity in space.

The deployment of weapons of mass destruction in space and on celestial bodies is prohibited already by an international treaty. In recent years, however, there have been signs that other types of military activities in space, which raise troubling questions, are being considered. According to US officials, the Soviet Union has developed and tested since 1977 an operational system capable of destroying satellites in particular orbits. The Soviet Union, on the other hand, considers the US space shuttle to be capable of becoming an effective anti-satellite system. Developments of these kinds raise fears that in case of war one side might attack the other's communications and warning satellites, thereby making a retaliatory attack more difficult and less reliable. Such fears could aggravate crises and make war more likely. In peacetime, knowledge that the adversary is carrying out such programmes and might soon deploy an operational system raises suspicions, contributing to deteriorating political relations.

The US and USSR held talks between 1977 and 1979 on the possibility of an agreement to prohibit the development and deployment of anti-satellite weapons, and the dismantling of existing systems. The Commission endorses these talks and urges their resumption and the rapid conclusion of an agreement.

There also has been speculation that the great powers may soon consider additional military uses of space, some of which would

123

raise new concerns and new threats. For example, there is speculation that in the future it may be possible to deploy weapons in space, making use of directed energy beams, as anti-ballistic missile systems. The Commission considers that such further militarization of space would constitute a dangerous expansion of military competition. We urge that countries begin discussions to restrict military research leading to the development of weapons for use in space, including possible directed energy weapons. We also urge that countries give serious consideration to proposals under discussion in the UN and other fora to prevent the further militarization of space.

Chemical and biological weapons
Renewed competition in chemical and biological weapons would be one of the most disturbing consequences of a broadened qualitative competition in armaments. Yet, increasingly, there are signs of renewed interest in these weapons. This is one area of the arms race in which it should be possible to make immediate and comprehensive strides towards disarmament. In fact, it is morally reprehensible not to make such progress rapidly.

Chemical weapon programmes are typically cloaked in secrecy, perhaps reflecting the nearly universal abhorrence for these weapons and those who would produce and use them. It is known that many types of lethal chemical agents have been developed and produced, including variants of the so-called contact gasses, an early form which was used during the First World War, and even more deadly, and now more common, nerve gasses.

The United States reports that it produced lethal chemical agents during and following the Second World War, but stopped all production in 1969. Recently, the US administration requested funds from the Congress to begin production of a new type of chemical weapon known as binary munitions.

The Soviet Union does not discuss the status of its chemical weapons production publicly. Some Western sources maintain that the Soviet Union has continued to produce lethal chemical agents throughout the 1970s.

Many types of munitions can be filled with lethal chemical agents, including bombs and other air-dropped munitions, the

124

warheads of surface-to-surface missiles, and artillery shells. Lethal chemical agents can also be sprayed by aircraft in a manner similar to crop-dusting. Virtually all these munitions are fired or delivered by the same weapon systems which fire conventional and sometimes nuclear ordnance. The great variety of chemical munitions and the commonality of delivery systems are among the problems which would make the verification of a treaty banning the production, stockpiling, and use of these weapons difficult. The similarities between plants used to produce lethal chemical agents and commercial chemical factories are a second problem.

It is clearly the case that existing agreements proscribing chemical and biological warfare are inadequate to assure signatories that they are being observed strictly by all parties. A number of suggestions have been made for clarifying questions of compliance, thus easing a corrosive factor in political relations. These include the establishment of a permanent consultative body with a technical staff under UN auspices, the creation of a standing consultative commission composed of the great powers and modelled after the body of the same name created by the 1972 Treaty Limiting Anti-Ballistic Missile Systems, and the convening of less formal organizations, as necessary, largely in diplomatic channels. Each of these ideas has merit and deserves consideration.

Beyond the strengthening of current agreements, it also would be desirable to conclude an agreement which called for the destruction of all existing stocks of chemical weapons, prohibited the production of such weapons in the future, and required the dismantling of existing production facilities. Any such agreement would have to include verification measures adequate to assure all signatories that the others were complying with its terms. For the most part, verification could rely on national technical means, but there also would have to be such cooperative measures as the declaration of production facilities and stocks, the possibility of on-site inspections on a challenge basis, the verification of the destruction of existing stocks by automatic devices, and international safeguards to assure developing nations that their interests also were being observed. The Commission urges in the strongest terms the Committee on Disarmament to continue its efforts to

125

formulate such a treaty, and the immediate resumption of US–Soviet negotiations on a comprehensive ban on chemical weapons.

The Third World dimension

There is a special Third World dimension to common security. Since 1945, wars have been waged frequently on the territories of Third World countries; according to one source, no fewer than 120 in seventy-one countries by 1971.[42] Like the major military powers, and often with their encouragement, Third World countries have been placing increasing reliance on the acquisition of arms as a means of trying to acquire security. There are powerful domestic factors behind this trend stemming primarily from the fear that their fragile sense of nationhood could be torn apart by internal tensions and instabilities. Matters are made worse when, as is sometimes the case, sustaining nationhood is a euphemism for sustaining regimes that have lost, or never had, a national consensus to govern.

Moreover, a very large proportion of Third World countries are small states; so small, indeed, that for them – and for the international community – whole new questions of security arise. The Third World now includes some sixty-two states with populations of less than one million, thirty-six of which have populations below 200,000. Their very smallness and weakness tempts others to pursue territorial and political ambitions through military interventions.

There is little doubt that the fear of external threats is a major reason for Third World arms purchases. Prominent among the causes of these threats are border disputes. If Third World countries are to be persuaded to participate in any comprehensive disarmament programme the international community must find creative ways of responding to their security concerns. This is a necessary precondition if the present escalation of Third World military expenditures is to be contained. Further reductions would then depend on the progress individual countries were able to make towards building internal stability – a process that might itself be assisted by the more rapid pace of economic development which a decline in arms purchases would facilitate.

126

Against this background of Third World needs and the record of Third World conflicts, an important focus of our work has been to explore whether, and to what extent, the present character of international relations can be modified. Total escape from it is impossible without the creation of a sovereign supranational authority, a not very likely prospect. Nevertheless, to accept that the security dilemma cannot be totally banished does not mean it cannot be ameliorated.

The international community, fulfilling its duties under the UN Charter, has in many ways helped to bring Third World states to nationhood. It has a further duty, within the spirit and expectation of the Charter, to foster an environment of material and psychological security. We believe that to a significant degree these special needs of Third World countries can be met. Moreover, we feel that this can be accomplished largely within the framework of existing international and regional institutions and mechanisms, principally by strengthening the role of the United Nations on the basis of partnership between the great powers and the other members.

Weakness of the UN's present security role

The UN's security role, as it has evolved, bears little relation to the original concept enshrined in the Charter. At its founding, the UN's most publicized advantage over its predecessor, the League of Nations, was that it was an international organization 'with teeth'. The linchpin of its authority was Chapter VII – 'action with respect to the peace, breaches of the peace, and acts of aggression'. Articles 39 to 51 of the Charter established a framework for collective security based on the use of military forces and provided the Security Council with authority for enforcement. The 1947 Report of the Military Staff Committee elaborated the technical requirements for enforcement actions: trained units earmarked for UN service and provided with adequate support, with the capacity to deter war and enforce the peace. But the political and military confrontation between East and West put this key chapter into limbo, where it remains to this day. The Military Staff Committee report was not accepted and its recommendations never implemented.

In place of the active collective security role envisaged in 1945, there has developed instead the more limited role known as 'peacekeeping'. The Commission readily acknowledges the valuable service which has been rendered by peacekeeping operations. They have prevented the escalation of a number of dangerous crises, notably in the Middle East. But their limitations are equally manifest. They can only be launched after a conflict has broken out. Their primary purpose is to maintain an effective ceasefire between two warring parties along the line of military control established by hostilities. They cannot be initiated except with the consent of all the warring parties. They required the mandate of the Security Council which may not be forthcoming because of political differences among the permanent members. They are accompanied by no sustained pressure for withdrawal from occupied territories, or for resolving the conflict in general, and can even become a guarantor of the gains of aggression. And they suffer further from an absence of any automatic and obligatory mechanism for their financing.

There are important lessons to be learnt about the roles and limits of the United Nations from the areas of tension and conflict in the world today: the Middle East, El Salvador, Afghanistan, Iran/Iraq, and Argentina and Britain in the Southern Atlantic, among others.

One area of particular concern, for example, is the insecurity that prevails in Southern Africa as a result of the continued failure to reach agreement on an appropriate UN settlement for an independent Namibia. South Africa has not only consistently placed obstacles in the way of reaching such a settlement but has used this ongoing unresolved situation as an excuse to mount armed incursions into the territories of neighbouring states like Angola, on the pretext of rounding up 'terrorists' working against the existing Namibian regime. The UN is seized with the Namibian problem by the common consent of all the member states, including South Africa. Yet it has no means currently at its disposal to deter South Africa from engaging in aggressive ventures which make a mockery of attempts to negotiate a peaceful solution.

In short, current concepts of peacekeeping possess little capacity to deter, cannot be invoked to prevent armed conflict, and therefore provide no alternative to the perceived need of Third World countries to build up independent military capabilities. In the absence of effective and reliable international machinery to safeguard their security, their sense of vulnerability will continue to increase, and with it their purchases of conventional arms and the heightened risks of conflict that such arms build-ups produce.

The sense of insecurity felt by Third World countries has been exacerbated by the competition among the great powers for influence. The Non-Aligned Movement, itself a manifestation of the desire of many developing countries to distance themselves from the effects of great power rivalry, has contributed a measure of confidence in the developing world but has not diminished the need for an effective global framework for collective security. In its absence, the Third World's disillusionment with the ability of the UN to contribute meaningfully to international peace and security will persist and they will continue to arm for survival.

The regional security dimension
Partly as a result of steadily eroding confidence in effective UN action and partly because of a desire among Third World countries to seek solutions to their problems free of great power interference, in recent years a tendency has developed to try to resolve conflicts at regional or sub-regional levels. For the most part, however, these efforts have been seriously hindered by political differences among the states of the region concerned and by financial problems. Their successes have been few. Yet, a strong disposition persists in favour of regional or sub-regional solutions whenever possible. And there are instances when regional approaches have provided a constructive beginning towards solutions as, for example, in the case of the Organization of African Unity (OAU) peacekeeping operation in Chad. There will therefore be continuing validity in regional initiatives, provided the regional organizations themselves are strengthened and their own security initiatives tied in with a more forceful UN security system.

But regional efforts, valuable as they may be, cannot become a substitute for the UN and its global responsibilities. Rather, each should reinforce the other. There is a particular need to develop cooperative procedures between the UN and Third World regional organizations designed to enlist UN financial and logistical assistance to bolster regional security arrangements.

The approaches adopted to strengthen regional organizations

129

must be tailored to the specific conditions and circumstances of the particular area. The various regions and sub-regions of the world differ widely with respect to their histories, local rivalries, and the involvement of external military powers, to say nothing of their current state of armament. Regional security arrangements, if they are to be viable, must be the result of an initiative from within the region and command the support of the large majority of regional countries. This may be difficult to achieve in those areas where there are major discrepancies in national power and wealth or conflicting interests relevant to the dispute under consideration, or where no properly representative regional organizations have been established. The Organization of American States, for example, not only includes one of the great powers, but excludes some Latin American countries on political grounds. No comprehensive regional organization exists in Asia or is likely to be established in the foreseeable future. Africa is thus the only region where, through the Organization of African Unity, regional security arrangements could at present be pursued effectively. However, the Chad experience itself underscores the practical financial difficulties of the OAU, the majority of whose members are too poor to fund such operations adequately. Moreover, it reinforces our belief in the value of devising cooperative financial and logistical arrangements between the world body and regional organizations.

Regardless of the means adopted, a more effective role for regional organizations could contribute to international peace and security by providing a framework and mechanism for the prevention, or at least containment, and resolution of local conflicts. Stronger regional organizations also could improve the capacity of the countries in a region or sub-region to withstand pressure from outside powers, thus reducing opportunities for the latter to aggravate local conflicts or disrupt intra-regional relations. By the same token, this could serve the interests of the major powers, helping them to withstand pressure from inside a region to become involved in a local dispute and reducing the risk of extending the geographical area of potential East–West confrontation.

Regional security issues cannot be resolved in isolation from shared economic problems. Peace and prosperity are two sides of the same coin. Economic circumstances often aggravate conflicts, both between nations and within nations. And economic policies are sometimes used to coerce neighbouring adversaries or reward friends. Thus, regional approaches must deal not only with security issues, but also with the economic problems which are influenced by, and in turn can have a decisive impact on, problems of war and peace.

Strengthening the UN's security role

In the final analysis, it is essential to develop a relevant and upgraded security role for the UN itself. We consider it imperative for the international community to bridge the huge gap between the active collective security concept envisaged by the Charter and the limited peacekeeping role that has evolved in its place. The solution must be responsive both to Third World security needs and the wider need to moderate great power rivalry in Third World disputes. The overwhelming majority of wars since 1945 have been fought between Third World countries. In a large number of cases, the great powers have been involved on opposite sides of these conflicts. In many of them no vital great power interests have been directly at stake. Yet, because of the absence of any kind of collective security machinery, the UN has been unable to act to deter or resolve these conflicts.

The collective security role originally envisaged for the UN can be partially revived, but only in circumstances where political consensus is possible among the great powers, on the one hand, and between them and the rest of the international community, on the other. Such political agreement is essential if a credible framework for collective security is to be established on which Third World countries could rely, and which would be free of the hit-and-miss character of peacekeeping operations. In short, the starting point must be a convergence of Third World and great power interests: the wish of Third World countries to settle disputes free of great power interference and a corresponding wish of the great powers not to become involved in armed confrontation arising out of Third World disputes. In particular, collective security must be free of any implications of great power hegemony or spheres of influence.

A start towards collective security

The Commission believes that border disputes could provide an immediate starting point.* Such disputes, which are mainly the legacy of the colonial era, are widespread throughout the Third World – in Africa, Asia, and Latin America. They are too numerous to list. Some have caused wars. Even where there has been no armed conflict, fears of attack by irredentist neighbours have fuelled defence expenditure that otherwise might have been avoided. And there is the likelihood that new border disputes will emerge from the creation of exclusive economic zones in former international waters.

We believe there should be a commitment within the international community in favour of invoking collective security procedures whenever a border dispute threatens or provokes an armed conflict between two or more Third World countries. Such an approach would give expression to the universally accepted international norm of respect for the territorial integrity of states. This is not only embodied in the Charter, but has been reaffirmed explicitly in important regional instruments such as the OAU Charter and the Final Act of the Helsinki Conference. It is, moreover, a basic tenet of the Non-Aligned Movement.

Indeed, we would go further and urge international agreement in support of collective security operations for all Third World disputes which are likely to cause, or actually result in, a breach of the peace – it being clearly understood that the decision to initiate collective security action would not prejudge the substantive issues causing the conflict. Activation of the collective security mechanism would therefore not require the Security Council to take an agreed posture on the merits of a given dispute, but would be simply a decision to ensure respect for the principle that invasion of territory and the settlement of disputes by force were not permissible. On this basis, political differences among members of the Security Council need not prevent collective security measures in specific Third World situations.

The certain knowledge that UN standby forces exist for certain purposes, and that they would be deployed if a violation of territory were threatened or took place in a Third World country, would in itself act as a major deterrent to would-be aggressors. Equally important, the creation of an enforcement capability would open

---

* With the possible exception of the Middle East, which is *sui generis*.

up a range of new possibilities for the Security Council and the UN Secretary General to initiate preventive actions, both diplomatic and military, to head off threatened armed conflicts.

If these procedures are to be effective and serve the cause of disarmament in the Third World, it must be understood universally that they would without doubt be brought into play – both to prevent conflict and to enforce its settlement. For this purpose, states should be committed in advance to accept such actions, and the permanent members of the Security Council should solemnly agree to a kind of 'political concordat' to support it, at least to the extent of not voting against it. The cooperation of the permanent members of the Security Council is particularly important. Their consent is a basic prerequisite for the effective functioning of the UN system. Their active cooperation is of special significance in dealing with threats to international peace and security.

Our proposal does not seek to vest sovereignty in the UN, or create any kind of supranational authority. It is designed to take account of the vastly different international community which has resulted from the decolonization process. The UN has played a key role in that process, but it has not been able to protect these new countries from 'the scourge of war'. The new nations of the world are rightly jealous of their sovereignty. We do not seek to curb or restrain it. We do, however, feel it is incumbent on all states, old and new, seeing themselves as component parts of an essentially interdependent society, to create voluntary mechanisms to harmonize their sovereignty and interdependence in a heavily armed world. Our proposal is a first step in this direction.

The question may be asked, Why limit collective security measures to Third World disputes? In theory, there can be no objection to a global approach. Practicality, however, dictates otherwise. Disputes beyond the Third World invariably involve NATO or Warsaw Pact countries. The East–West conflict has prevented the development of international collective security in the past. It retains the potential to frustrate its evolution still. More directly, the concordat proposed as an important element in facilitating an international regime of collective security would likely not be forthcoming were the initial proposals global in their reach. This is one of those cases where much that would be beneficial could remain undone if we allowed the best to become

133

the enemy of the good. But there is a further point. A successful start with collective security on a pragmatic, if not universal, basis may well provide all countries with the confidence necessary to take further steps at some later time.

If our proposal is implemented, we see significant benefits accruing not only to the Third World but to the international community as a whole. An important step would have been taken to diminish the insecurity that now characterizes international relations, to foster a new framework of cooperation between the great powers from which there could be other spin-offs in the long term, to create confidence in the UN system, to facilitate lower levels of defence expenditure in Third World countries and thereby greatly advance their prospects of economic development. These would be substantial gains.

Arms negotiations and verification

In one sense, it is extraordinary that hostile nations can sit together and negotiate limitations on the weapons which they perceive to lie at the heart of their security. It is a rare phenomenon historically. It should thus not surprise us that these talks have progressed only slowly. Each side has circled the other warily, with doubts and suspicions the rule.

The secrecy which normally cloaks military establishments has complicated these talks. Arms negotiators discuss with their adversaries things they sometimes do not mention to their own citizens. Secrecy also makes it difficult to explain and gain support for agreements that result from negotiations.

The technologies used to monitor military capabilities in foreign nations have advanced impressively over the past thirty years. The development and routine operation of earth satellites, greater knowledge in many sciences, advances in miniaturized electronics, and startling progess in systems used to process large quantities of data rapidly and reliably have provided to several nations the means of observing, analysing, and assessing with relative confidence both the size and structure of the armed forces of potential adversaries and the performance characteristics of weapon systems.

Science has not made military establishments transparent,

however. Even in the knowledge of the most scientifically advanced nations, and even as concerns the military establishments that publish abundant information, many uncertainties remain. These uncertainties often raise serious doubts about the intentions of potential adversaries. Better knowledge about rival states leads to more accurate and less ominous forecasts of future developments.

It is thus desirable for nations to make available as many essential facts about their military capabilities – both present and prospective – as possible. Regular exchanges of information with the community of nations help to erode international suspicions.

Obviously, whatever is done in this regard must be consistent with the requirements of national security. Also, the degree of secrecy is related to the political climate, as well as to traditions and histories of different nations. Greater openness is more likely at times of good relations than ones of tension.

Cooperation in facilitating the acquisition of information about opposing military forces is most important when considering specific agreements. Verifying compliance with arms agreements is always an uncertain process, but the degree of uncertainty can be reduced by measures which assist the use of national technical means. The more cooperative that parties to an agreement are in this respect, the less difficult are negotiations, and the more likely that the treaty can gain the support of political leaders in all states.

Equally important are steps to ensure that new weapons do not make the negotiation of verifiable arms agreements excessively difficult. Compliance with restrictions on weapon developments and deployments can be more or less difficult to monitor depending on the specific design of the weapon system. Mobile systems, smaller systems, weapon systems that serve multiple purposes, weapon systems that can be fitted with nuclear or conventional warheads, all can complicate the negotiation and verification of arms agreements. Verification problems will be less or more difficult to solve, depending on specific characteristics designed into the weapon.

Clearly, there is no all-purpose formula for determining the degree, or specific types, of cooperation which are necessary to verify arms agreements. There must be a close link between the scope and design of the treaty and the means specified to assure its verification; the two must be negotiated together. And the means of verification should be tailored to the significance of the agreement. The more deeply a treaty bites into existing arsenals or the more tightly it binds possible future developments of military technologies, the more comprehensive must be the means of verification specified in the agreement.

A few general rules are recognizable. *First*, a commitment to serious negotiations carries with it an obligation to provide the data necessary to facilitate negotiation and implementation of the agreement. There should be a close link, however, between the scope of the agreement and the amount of data that must be tabled at the negotiation. *Second*, parties to arms control agreements should always refrain from deliberately concealing the objects of that agreement. *Third*, consideration should always be given to providing a forum for discussing measures which raise concerns about compliance with the agreement. The Standing Consultative Commission established by the 1972 SALT agreements is an excellent example of such a body.

The Commission has examined carefully the question of verification. Foolproof verification is clearly unattainable and insistence thereon would only make agreements impossible. Violation of an agreement based on adequate verification of compliance would entail a risk of detection, and therefore a danger of jeopardizing the agreement in question and political relations among the parties to the treaty. If agreements reflect mutual interests a violation of them would amount to a violation of self-interest. From this perspective, the Commission emphasizes the need for adequate verification.

Beyond these basic rules, means of assuring the verification of an agreement must be tailored to the treaty itself. In many cases, parties can rely solely on their own national technical means. In other cases, 'cooperative measures' are necessary. The agreement in SALT II not to encrypt certain data transmitted back to earth during missile tests is an example of a non-intrusive cooperative measure. In still other cases, more far-reaching cooperative means, such as the establishment of unmanned devices on the territory of signatories, may be necessary. And in other instances, inspections by one side of certain objects on the territory of the other would be necessary. Any such arrangement should be as limited as possible, but on-site inspections should not be ruled out in principle.

Judgements about the verifiability of arms control arrangements reflect political decisions. Like any such judgement, they can be hampered or facilitated by the general character of relations between the signatories, and by specific measures which aim to enhance the prospects for favourable consideration.

Finally, confidence- and security-building measures can also help to create an atmosphere in which more rapid progress towards arms limitation and disarmament becomes possible. These measures could decrease fears of surprise attack, as well as make it more difficult to exploit military advantages for political gain. Confidence-building measures also would be natural adjuncts to agreements that specified reductions in military forces. They could help to ease suspicions and the pressures from extreme elements which sometimes lead nations to withdraw from or terminate agreements, and at all times poison the atmosphere for greater progress in the future.

The exchange of data describing particular types of military force is one way to initiate a process of building greater mutual confidence in the defensive orientation of respective military forces. Restrictions on certain types of military activity in certain locations also could contribute to a better atmosphere. The 1972 US–Soviet agreement concerning the operation of naval vessels, for example, seems to have worked effectively in reducing the tensions previously associated with provocative manoeuvres by opposing fleets during difficult political circumstances.

In the future, in a cooperative political atmosphere, the exchange of military observers could be an effective way of assuring rival nations that no untoward military actions were being contemplated. Similar functions could be accomplished with automatic devices. The major nuclear powers could implant unmanned devices in each other's missile fields to provide warning of launches and therefore greater confidence that an attack could not occur without maximum warning.

Measures like these could be helpful in building confidence that all nations were adhering to the basic assumptions of common security; that despite their ideological and political differences they were prepared to cooperate for their common benefit.

6 Recommendations and proposals

A new departure

We are deeply concerned about trends in the development, deployment, and proliferation of armaments. They are exacerbated by the deterioration in political relations. Unless states manage to reverse them, the world may be heading for catastrophe. Preventive action is therefore needed urgently. The problems we confront are man-made problems. Humanity has it within its power to contain the dangers and embark upon a programme for the reduction and eventual abolition of the forces of destruction. The efforts so far have been too feeble and their results too meagre for this Commission to recommend merely renewed commitment and enhanced endeavour. More of the same will not do. We recognize the constraints which apply, the competing interests and mutual suspicions which permeate international relations. We see the need for a new beginning in the peaceful struggle against war and destruction.

Principles for action

Common security

All states have a right to security. In the absence of a world authority with the right and power to police international relations, states have to protect themselves. Unless they show mutual restraint and proper appreciation of the realities of the nuclear age, however, the pursuit of security can cause intensified competition and more tense political relations and, at the end of the day, a reduction in security for all concerned.

Nuclear weapons have changed not only the scale of warfare but the very concept of war itself. In the nuclear age war cannot be an instrument of policy, only an engine for unprecedented destruction.

States can no longer seek security at each other's expense; it can be attained only through cooperative undertakings. Security in the nuclear age means common security. Even ideological opponents and political rivals have a shared interest in survival. There must be partnership in the struggle against war itself. The search for arms control and disarmament is the pursuit of common gains, not unilateral advantage. *A doctrine of common security must replace the present expedient of deterrence through armaments. International peace must rest on a commitment to joint survival rather than a threat of mutual destruction.*

General and complete disarmament
In its final document, the first special session of the General Assembly devoted to disarmament charged the Committee on Disarmament with elaborating a comprehensive programme leading to general and complete disarmament. The Committee completed its task in April 1982. *The Commission strongly supports the goal of general and complete disarmament.* We recognize that this objective will not be realized in the near future. But the ideal of a world in which international relations are based on the rule of law, cooperation, and the peaceful pursuit of political ends must be held high. This is the goal as well as the measure of efforts to reach international agreements on arms limitation and disarmament. To make progress in that direction it is necessary to develop a concrete and comprehensive programme of action reflecting the complex interrelationships of the many critical elements in the present situation. It is necessary to break the impasse and start a downward spiral.

Economic pressures and common security
The economic and social costs of military competition constitute strong reasons for countries to seek disarmament. The costs of military spending are especially onerous in the difficult economic circumstances of the 1980s. These costs, of course, are different for different countries. But some are common to almost everyone: use of government revenues; diversion of scarce scientific and technical skills from social pursuits; denial of investments which could otherwise increase economic growth. The journey towards reversing the arms race will follow a different path for each

139

country. But for all countries the economic prize will be great.

Linkage as an obstacle

The Commission is disturbed by the current international situation. Dialogue and moderation appear to be breaking down; tensions are accelerating. While weapons are not the only source of conflict among states, competitions in arms exacerbate existing conficts and assume a dangerous and self-propelling momentum.

Deliberate efforts to establish links between specific negotiations for the limitation and reduction of arms and the general international behaviour of one's opponent are inconsistent with our notion of common security. Negotiations for the limitation and reduction of arms require a high degree of continuity and stability. They are not gifts to an adversary or rewards for his good behaviour, but rather a means of pursuing common security and profiting from shared interests. The task of diplomacy is to limit, split, and subdivide conflicts, not to generalize and aggregate them. Prior political agreement cannot be made a precondition for negotiations about arms limitation. Indeed, agreements on arms limitation and disarmament could make it easier to resolve outstanding issues. *The Commission considers the notion of political linkage an unsound principle which should be abandoned.*

The prospects for arms limitation and disarmament will to some extent always depend on the general political climate. However, all states share an interest in preventing the arms race from dominating their relations and driving them towards armed conflict. Negotiations about, and agreements to limit and reduce, arms can provide an engine for improving relations and restoring confidence. When tensions occur the need for communication and negotiation is particularly strong.

Elements of a programme for arms control and disarmament

The Commission's recommendations, taken together, constitute a broad programme for substantial progress towards arms limitation and disarmament. The recommendations fall into six categories: (1) the nuclear challenge and East–West relations; (2) curbing the

140

qualitative arms competition; (3) assuring confidence among states; (4) strengthening the UN security system; (5) regional approaches to security; and (6) economic security.

1 The nuclear challenge and East–West relations

There will be no winner in a nuclear war. The use of nuclear weapons would result in devastation and suffering of a magnitude which would render meaningless any notion of victory. The size of existing nuclear stockpiles and the near certainty of devastating retaliation make it futile and dangerous to consider nuclear war an instrument of national policy. Nuclear war would amount to an unprecedented catastrophe for humanity and suicide for those who resorted to it.

No victors in a nuclear war

Were they ever to cross the nuclear threshold, nations would be set on a course which does not lend itself to prediction. The very process of destruction would render prior calculations and attempts to exercise control fruitless. We reject any notion of 'windows of opportunity' for nuclear war. Any doctrine based on the belief that it may be possible to wage a victorious nuclear war is a dangerous challenge to the prudence and responsibility which must inspire all approaches to international peace and security in the nuclear age. *We conclude that it is impossible to win a nuclear war and dangerous for states to pursue policies or strategies based on the fallacious assumption that a nuclear war might be won.*

No limited nuclear war

The idea of fighting a limited nuclear war is dangerous. Nuclear weapons are not war-fighting weapons. Once the nuclear threshold had been crossed the dynamics of escalation would inexorably propel events towards catastrophe. Doctrines and strategies of limited nuclear war thus carry dangerous connotations. Their acceptance would diminish the fears and perceived risks of nuclear war and blur the distinction between nuclear and 'conventional' armed conflict, thus lowering the nuclear threshold.

Even if it is understood that nuclear war cannot be controlled, nations would feel compelled to attempt to limit war should it begin. Paradoxically, preparations for such contingencies, manifested in the acquisition of certain weapons and control systems, can be dangerous to the extent that they may be interpreted as suggesting the possibility of fighting a limited nuclear war as a matter of deliberate policy.

Deterrence cannot be made foolproof. It could collapse in many different ways: because of a technical accident, a human error or miscalculation, the snowballing effect of a local conflict, among others. Nations must guard against these possibilities through cooperative agreements for emergency communications. But they also must abandon doctrines and preparations for fighting limited nuclear war as a matter of deliberate policy.

Nuclear deterrence cannot provide the long-term basis for peace, stability, and equity in international society. It must be replaced by the concept of common security.

The conclusion is therefore inevitably that nuclear weapons must be eliminated. We are fully aware, however, that this can only be achieved through a gradual process which must be initiated by concrete steps.

1.1 Reductions and qualitative limitations of nuclear forces

Nuclear weapons are part of the established reality. The nuclear arms race continues. In a very real sense a nuclear shadow hangs over all political and armed conflicts in the contemporary age. Most disturbing is the development and deployment of weapons which may lead to a lowering of the nuclear threshold with the attendant increased risk of nuclear war. The greatest danger would be for people anywhere to become so used to an open-ended nuclear arms race that they become complacent about the danger involved, or lose faith in their capacity to turn the tide. But nations are not condemned to live by the ugly dictates of nuclear weapons. They have the choice and indeed the responsibility to curb and eliminate the horrendous forces of destruction which nuclear weapons represent.

We believe that there is an urgent need for agreements specifying major reductions of nuclear weapons and restraints on their qualitative improvements, with a view to maintaining parity at the lowest possible level of forces. Stabilizing the nuclear arms race in this way could create a basis for further steps in the direction of

142

stopping the production of nuclear weapons and reaching agreement on their eventual elimination. There is a need to create a downward momentum. Nations cannot confine their efforts to managing the existing high levels of armaments. Major reductions and constraints on qualitative 'improvements' must be a dominant theme in future negotiations and agreements.

1.2 Reductions and qualitative limitations in US and USSR strategic forces

Nuclear deterrence can be but a temporary expedient. It provides no permanent solution to international security. The consequences of failure are too terrifying to leave the system unchanged. The world must break with a system which equates the maintenance of peace with holding millions of human beings and the fruits of their labour as hostages for the good behaviour of the governments of the nuclear weapon states.

The process of strategic arms limitation therefore is indispensable. It is important, too, because it has become a key factor in the relations between the United States and the Soviet Union, affecting the very framework and climate of international relations. The 1972 and 1979 SALT agreements constitute an important beginning; they must be preserved and the process continued to provide a downward spiral in nuclear arms.

Negotiations must be resumed without precondition and further delay. The objective of the negotiations must be twofold: *First, the parties should reaffirm the important limitations and restraints that the SALT II Treaty provides, and agree on any necessary clarifications or adjustments of the Treaty in that connection. Second, the parties should seek a follow-on treaty providing for major reductions and qualitative limitations resulting in essential parity at substantially lower and more stable levels of forces. Particular emphasis should be accorded to reductions and qualitative limitations that would reduce fears of a 'first strike', an attempt to disarm an opponent or to forestall a possible attack by a preemptive surprise attack. Any new agreement should also contain provisions necessary to assure adequate verification of these reductions and qualitative limitations, and should prohibit deployment of weapon systems which would circumvent agreed limitations and reductions or render verification impossible.*

143

Successive agreements should point to the eventual elimination of strategic nuclear arms through interim stages that restrict the arsenals of the nuclear weapon states to small, secure strategic forces in consonance with the principle of equal security.

1.3 The anti-ballistic missile treaty must be upheld

The 1972 Treaty Limiting Anti-Ballistic Missile Systems is an important agreement designed to lessen the chance of nuclear war and to constrain the strategic arms race from escalating into broader dimensions. It does not suggest that international peace and security should be based on the ability of the great powers to inflict unacceptable destruction on each other. It does reflect the fact that for the foreseeable future there are no effective means of defending against ballistic missiles. States must coexist, therefore, in a condition of mutual vulnerability, making the pursuit of common security a matter of survival for humanity.

The Anti-Ballistic Missile Treaty is a substantial and necessary building block in a viable system of common security. Abrogation of the Treaty would undermine the whole strategic arms limitation and reduction process. *The failure to uphold the Anti-Ballistic Missile Treaty could lead to a destabilization of the international situation and a greater risk of nuclear war. We urge that the treaty be upheld.*

1.4 Parity in conventional forces in Europe should be established at lower levels

The major military confrontation between East and West is in Europe and takes place between NATO and the Warsaw Pact. The concentration of military power assembled in Europe is the greatest in history. The Commission recognizes the complex inter-relationships which exist among the various elements of the armed forces on both sides, nuclear and conventional, as well as between the force postures of the two alliances. A fair appraisal of the East–West balance of forces on the continent of Europe is extremely complicated. So many aspects of economy, geography, technology, traditions, military organization, and threat perceptions are involved. A comprehensive approach to arms limitation and reductions must be adopted in order to assure approximate military parity at substantially reduced levels and to reduce the risk of nuclear war.

We are convinced that a large-scale conventional war in densely populated Europe would be enormously destructive and in all likelihood would escalate to the nuclear level. It would affect not only the nuclear weapon states or allied states, but also neutral and non-aligned countries. War is not an acceptable option for the resolution of political conflict in the nuclear age. *The armies which are poised against each other in Europe today are much larger than would be necessitated by realistic appraisals of basic security needs. Common security would be enhanced by drastic mutual reductions.*

Since 1973 the two alliances in Europe have been negotiating in Vienna about an agreement on mutual force reductions in Central Europe. They have reached consensus on most of the basic principles that would govern an agreement. It would provide for reductions in two phases leading to equal collective ceilings of 900,000 men, a subceiling of 700,000 for land-force personnel in the reduction area, and associated measures designed to ensure compliance with the provisions of the agreement and to enhance both sides' confidence. The parties have still to agree on what is the number of troops in the reduction area at the present time, the details of the linkage between the two phases of reductions, and the scope of the associated measures. The Commission considers that the outstanding differences could be resolved satisfactorily provided there were the political will to do so. Continued stalemate will seriously diminish public confidence in negotiations for arms reductions. *We urge that the participating states convene a meeting of Foreign Ministers to resolve the differences and conclude an agreement before the end of 1982.*

An agreement specifying parity and reduction of conventional forces in Central Europe should be accompanied by commitments to abstain from moving arms and troops to areas where they would diminish the security of other countries in Europe. Agreement in Vienna on conventional forces in Central Europe would provide a basis for, and facilitate the negotiation of, agreements on withdrawal and reduction of nuclear weapons in Europe. A subsequent agreement on parity of conventional forces in Europe

145

at substantially reduced levels could facilitate more far-reaching agreements on the withdrawal and reduction of nuclear weapons. Such agreements would be more likely if in the negotiations for conventional force reductions the parties were to emphasize reducing those elements of the two sides' military postures which the parties consider the most threatening.

1.5 Reducing the nuclear threat in Europe

The nuclear arsenals in Europe are awesome. Furthermore, the Commission is deeply concerned about those nuclear postures and doctrines which dangerously and erroneously suggest that it may be possible to fight and 'win' a limited nuclear war. In the event of a crisis their effect could be to drive the contending forces across the threshold of a nuclear war. The Commission is convinced that there must be substantial reductions in the nuclear stockpile leading to denuclearization in Europe and eventually to a world free of nuclear weapons. A necessary precondition is a negotiated agreement on substantial mutual force reductions establishing and guaranteeing an approximate parity of conventional forces between the two major alliances.

Therefore, *the Commission supports a negotiated agreement for approximate parity in conventional forces between the two alliances. Such an agreement would facilitate reductions in nuclear weapons and a reordering of the priority now accorded to nuclear arms in military contingency planning.*

The Commission has devoted much time and effort to examining various alternative ways for bringing these changes about.* Among the alternatives studied was nuclear-weapon-free zones, which are dealt with in Section 5.3 concerning regional security arrangements. It should be remembered in this connection that some countries in Europe do not belong to any of the military alliances and have renounced the acquisition of nuclear arms.

Here we propose a functional approach concentrating on specific weapons and classes of weapon. *Our proposal for the gradual removal of the nuclear threat posed to Europe includes establishment of a battlefield-nuclear-weapon-free zone and measures to strengthen the nuclear threshold and reduce pressures*

---

*See Annexe Two: Comment by Egon Bahr.

for the early use of nuclear weapons, and substantial reductions in all categories of intermediate- (medium-) and shorter-range nuclear weapons which threaten Europe.

(a) A battlefield-nuclear-weapon-free zone in Europe. We call special attention to the dangers posed by those nuclear weapons whose delivery systems are deployed in considerable numbers to forward positions in Europe. These are known as 'battlefield' nuclear weapons. A large portion of NATO's and the Warsaw Pact's nuclear munitions in Europe are of this type. The weapons are designed and deployed to provide support to ground forces in direct contact with the forces of the opponent. Their delivery systems have ranges up to 150 kilometres, and are primarily short-range rockets, mines, and artillery. Most of the delivery systems are dual-capable, i.e. they can fire either conventional munitions or nuclear munitions.

Because of their deployment in forward areas battlefield nuclear weapons run the risk of being overrun early in an armed conflict. Maintaining command and control over such weapons in 'the fog of war' would be difficult. Pressures for delegation of authority to use nuclear weapons to local commanders and for their early use would be strong. The danger of crossing the nuclear threshold and of further escalation could become acute. It should be remembered in this connection that the areas close to the East–West border in Central Europe are densely populated and contain large industrial concentrations.

The Commission recommends the establishment of a battlefield-nuclear-weapon-free zone, starting with Central Europe and extending ultimately from the northern to the southern flanks of the two alliances. This scheme would be implemented in the context of an agreement on parity and mutual force reductions in Central Europe. No nuclear munitions would be permitted in the zone.*

---

*Giorgi Arbatov expressed doubts about the arms control value of this proposal as nuclear munitions could be quickly reintroduced into the proscribed area. Such an agreement which is of small military significance would be difficult to negotiate, and could create an unfounded impression of enhanced security. In his opinion, other more effective measures are needed – radical reductions up to a complete ban of all medium-range and tactical nuclear weapons. This would amount to a genuine zero-option for Europe.

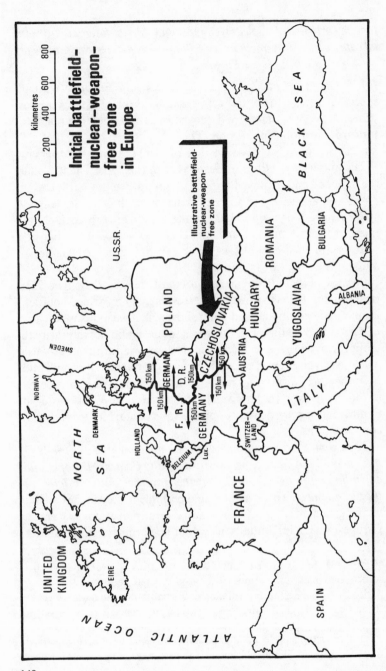

Initial battlefield-
nuclear-weapon-
free zone
in Europe

kilometres

0   200   400   600   800

Illustrative battlefield-
nuclear-weapon-
free zone

Storage sites for nuclear munitions also would be prohibited. Manoeuvres simulating nuclear operations would not be allowed in the zone. Preparations for the emplacement of atomic demolition munitions and storage of such weapons would be prohibited.

There also should be rules governing the presence in the zone of artillery and short-range missiles that could be adapted for both nuclear and conventional use. The geographic definition of the zone should be determined through negotiations, taking into account the relevant circumstances in the areas involved, but for illustrative purposes, a width of 150 kilometres on both sides may be suggested. Provisions for verifying compliance with these prohibitions would be negotiated. They would have to include a limited number of on-site inspections in the zone on a challenge basis.

The Commission recognizes that nuclear munitions may be brought back to the forward areas in wartime, and that nuclear weapons may be delivered by aircraft and other longer range systems. However, we consider the establishment of the proposed zone an important confidence-building measure which would raise the nuclear threshold and reduce some of the pressures for early use of nuclear weapons. It is consistent with our rejection of limited nuclear war as a matter of deliberate policy.

The agreement for withdrawal of 'battlefield' nuclear weapons from the forward zone should be followed by substantial reductions in the number of nuclear munitions in Europe with adequate measures of verification.

*(b) Maintain a clear nuclear threshold. To contain and reduce the danger of nuclear confrontation in Europe it is important to maintain a clear distinction between nuclear and conventional weapons. We urge the nuclear weapon states to abstain from deploying weapons which blur the distinction by appearing to be more 'useable'. The so-called 'mini-nukes' and enhanced radiation (neutron) weapons both fall into this category.**

---

*Robert Ford, David Owen, and Cyrus Vance comment as follows on the Commission's recommendations on enhanced radiation weapons: We do not advocate the deployment of such weapons at this time. We consider, however, that both in their asserted benefits for military effectiveness and in

149

(c) Reduction of intermediate- (medium-) range nuclear weapon systems. The Commission welcomes the opening of negotiations between the United States and the Soviet Union on intermediate-range nuclear weapons and urges the parties to give the search for agreement the highest priority. The competitive deployment of these weapons constitutes a serious blow to political and military stability between East and West, particularly in Europe. *Negotiations should reduce the number of all such weapons to essential parity at the lowest possible level, preferably at a level which would mean that NATO would forgo the introduction of a new generation of intermediate-range missiles in Europe.* Furthermore, we call on the parties also to *agree to a ban on deployment of new short-range nuclear weapon systems to areas from which they could threaten the same targets which are threatened by intermediate- (medium-) range nuclear weapons.*

In addition to an accord on intermediate-range nuclear weapons in Europe the parties should commit themselves to continue negotiations to limit all other nuclear forces which threaten Europe, including sea-based cruise missiles. All nuclear weapons which are deployed in or against Europe, including French and British forces, should be taken into consideration.*

1.6 A chemical-weapon-free zone in Europe

The world may be on the brink of a major new arms race in chemical weaponry. The Commission considers chemical weapons

---

their alleged adverse impact on the risk of nuclear war, any incremental effects of enhanced radiation weapons are relatively minor as compared to the basic problems raised by any nuclear weapon. A decision to initiate nuclear war, the most momentous decision any political leader would ever confront, would not be made more easily or more quickly because enhanced radiation weapons, rather than nuclear weapons of older design, were available for use.

---

*Joop den Uyl endorses the proposal of the Commission for the gradual removal of the nuclear threat to Europe. He maintains his conviction that an overall balance of nuclear arms does not require precise parity of nuclear weapons on every level and for every class of weapon. He re-affirms his opposition to the stationing of new nuclear weapon systems in NATO and Warsaw Pact countries.

particularly abhorrent, and condemns any use of such inhumane weapons.

Chemical weapons (including contact gasses and nerve agents) fall between, and share some of the characteristics of, both conventional and nuclear warfare. They may be dispensed from munitions adaptable to most types of conventional weapon system. They have indiscriminate and unpredictable effects due to weather. Some can persist, poisoning the environment for a long time. It has been estimated that if chemical weapons were used in densely populated Europe, the ratio of non-combatant to combatant casualties could be as high as twenty to one. Moreover, the use of chemical weapons would blur the distinction between conventional and nuclear warfare. This would increase the danger of one sliding into the other.

Chemical weapon stockpiles include both bulk storage containers for chemical agents from which munitions can be charged, and such munitions as artillery shells, rocket warheads, aerial bombs, and mines already loaded with chemical agents. Since they are highly toxic, special safety precautions are needed during storage and handling. This is why it is generally assumed that chemical weapons are stored in a small number of central depots in Europe. Information about the possible distribution of chemical weapons to troops in the field is both uncertain and contradictory. The development of so-called 'binary' munitions, however, could facilitate their distribution. These munitions are filled with two less toxic chemicals which are combined to create a lethal nerve gas only after the munition has been fired.

The Commission calls for the establishment of a chemical-weapon-free zone in Europe, beginning with Central Europe. The agreement would include a declaration of the whereabouts of existing depots and stockpiles in Europe, adequate means to verify their destruction, and procedures for monitoring compliance on a continuing basis, including a few on-site inspections on a challenge basis. The training of troops in the offensive use of chemical weapons also would be prohibited.

1.7 Confidence- and security-building measures in Europe

The Commission considers the Final Act of the 1975 Helsinki Conference on Security and Cooperation in Europe and the follow-up process important to the evolution of the security arrangements in Europe. It points beyond confrontation to cooperation and the pursuit of common security. A system of confidence-building measures relating to military manoeuvres has been instituted and adhered to by the participating states. In the follow-up meeting in Madrid, which will reconvene in November 1982, the participating states are negotiating the mandate for a Conference on Disarmament and Confidence and Security Building Measures. *The first phase would be devoted to negotiating agreement on Confidence and Security Building Measures which would apply to all of Europe, contribute to military security, be verifiable, and constitute a binding and lasting commitment. The Commission considers this effort an important contribution to the growth of a system and practice of common security in Europe. The second phase should comprise negotiations for substantial disarmament in Europe.*

2 Curbing the qualitative arms competition

Competitions in armaments focus as much on the characteristics of the weapons being acquired as on their number. Contrary to the principles of common security, states have sought to guarantee their survival and enhance their influence by developing or purchasing weapons that are more effective and lethal. The nuclear-weapon states continue to develop new kinds of nuclear weapons and new means of delivering them. They are searching for new means of warfare in space and other frontiers of human exploration. At the same time, a growing number of other states are increasing their potential to develop nuclear weapons at some future time.

All these developments aggravate existing political tensions among nations and make more difficult the avoidance and resolution of conflicts. The appearance of new types of military capabilities, no less than the appearance of greater numbers of weapons, can contribute to regional instability, raise fears of war and suspicion of hostile intentions. If nations are to live in common security, qualitative aspects of the arms race, like its quantitative features, must be constrained.

Advances in military capabilities begin in the human mind,

proceed in different strands in numerous offices and laboratories. Only when they are near completion do they coalesce in the concrete form of a new weapon. New applications of technology can sometimes be stabilizing, but more often they generate new instabilities and competitions. Large research and development establishments represent vested interests which generate pressures for further research and increased effort.

It is difficult to identify points in the process of military research and development at which nations could agree to exercise restraint and at which compliance with such agreements could be verified. The notable exception is the point at which prototypes of weapons are tested in the field. The possibility of restricting the development of new or improved weapon systems at this critical point should be utilized on a much more extensive scale. Indeed, agreements already have been reached which restrict qualitative aspects of arms competitions at the testing stage; the 1963 Partial Test Ban Treaty, the 1974 Threshold Test Ban Treaty, the 1972 Anti-Ballistic Missile Treaty, and the 1979 SALT II Treaty.

Moreover, just as in the case of quantitative limitations, nations are unlikely to be willing to exercise unreciprocated unilateral restraint for substantial periods. *The major nuclear-weapon states have a special responsibility, but all nations must seek qualitative restraints. Steps have to be taken in common by nuclear- and non-nuclear-weapon states, by arms exporters and arms purchasers, by East and West, by great powers and small states.*

2.1 A comprehensive test ban treaty

The conclusion of a treaty banning all nuclear tests would make the introduction of new weapon designs into the armories of the nuclear-weapon states much more difficult. It would be a major constraint on the qualitative development of more sophisticated nuclear weapons. It also could be an important contribution to limiting the improvement of the present stocks of nuclear weapons. Hence it would enhance the acceptability and credibility of the Non-Proliferation Treaty, which works to limit the spread of nuclear weapons.

The Commission considers that efforts should be concentrated on the negotiation of a treaty banning all nuclear tests. Such a treaty is needed in order to forestall a new round of nuclear weapon

153

developments which could exacerbate East–West relations, reduce stability, and weaken the Non-Proliferation Treaty.

The Commission welcomes the decision of the Committee on Disarmament in April 1982 to establish an *ad hoc* working group on a nuclear test ban. The Commission trusts that it will soon be possible to negotiate and conclude the Comprehensive Test Ban Treaty which for more than a quarter of a century has been awaited in vain by peoples the world over.

In further support thereof, we urge that the trilateral negotiations between the United States, the Soviet Union, and the United Kingdom on a comprehensive test ban be resumed immediately in order to settle the still unresolved issues, including the question of verification. Political will is needed in order to transcend the remaining obstacles. The Commission is of the view that it is possible to establish an effective system of verification and confidence building by arrangements involving the International Seismic Data Exchange, agreed procedures for consultation and on-site inspection, and a network of national seismic stations.

During the period between completion of negotiations and formal ratification of the test ban treaty, all the nuclear powers should participate in a voluntary moratorium on all nuclear tests.

2.2 A ban on anti-satellite systems
Outer space has become an important part of the military competition between East and West. The military machines of the major powers have become increasingly dependent on space-based support. Satellite systems have opened up a wide range of possibilities for verification and warning, for command, control, and communications. If these satellites were threatened, it could result in a substantial expansion of the strategic arms race into outer space, as each side sought to protect its own system.

Between 1977 and 1979 the Soviet Union and the United States discussed a ban on anti-satellite weapons. Time is running out. *The Commission recommends that these negotiations be reopened and that priority be given to a suspension and prohibition of the testing of anti-satellite weapons. It is essential that such a ban go into effect before irreversible technological 'progress' has been made. Negotions also should aim at reaching agreement that would ban the*

154

deployment of anti-satellite weapons and require the dismantling of existing systems.

Further bans on weapons and activities in outer space will undoubtedly be needed. The exploitation of outer space raises a number of complex technical questions and judgements. *The Commission urges the major industrial powers to develop a dialogue with the aim of identifying and preventing military uses of outer space that might constitute threats to international peace and security. This dialogue should lead to negotiated bans and limits on specific weapon systems or entire areas of activity.*

2.3 A chemical weapon disarmament treaty

The existing chemical and biological arms control and disarmament agreements are among the few safeguards against the dangers of an expanded arms race. Use in war of both chemical and biological weapons is prohibited by the 1925 Geneva Protocol and its associated body of customary international law. Possession of biological weapons, including toxin weapons, is outlawed by the 1975 Biological Weapons Convention. But the possession of chemical weapons is not prohibited and a number of states have reserved the right to use them if they are attacked with chemical weapons. The majority of states are parties to these agreements and have under the 1975 Convention committed themselves to continue negotiations 'in good faith' to prohibit possession of chemical weapons.

Since the First World War, chemical weapons have only been used in conflicts in the developing world. All reports of alleged use also are limited to Third World countries. Thus a new arms race in chemical weapons poses worldwide dangers, in particular for the developing world.

Pressures to build up stocks of chemical weapons are in danger of subverting the existing accords. *It is vital to accelerate negotiations aimed at extending and strengthening existing agreements by the introduction of a comprehensive chemical weapon disarmament treaty banning such weapons altogether.* This requires resumption of the stalled bilateral talks between the United States and the Soviet Union. When these negotiations last were convened, in July 1980, there was agreement in principle on the use of on-site inspection as a verification technique. Bilateral talks do not, of course, substitute for renewed efforts within the Committee on Disarmament to negotiate agreement on a comprehensive chemical weapon disarmament treaty, but would strengthen those efforts.

The negotiations involve complex technical matters and sensitive political issues and will require time to conclude successfully. Therefore *we call in addition for agreement on consultative procedures so that problems arising under the Geneva Protocol and the Biological Warfare Convention can be resolved through international cooperation. Such procedures could include the option of consultative meetings being convened at the expert level under the auspices of the United Nations that would be open to all states.*

A chemical weapon disarmament treaty should contain provisions for a permanent consultative commission composed of all the parties to the treaty and served by a small technical staff. The commission should ensure implementation of the treaty and thereafter monitor continued compliance. It could also be charged with the establishment of an effective complaint procedure.

Appropriate verification must be agreed for each stage of implementation of a treaty on chemical weapon disarmament. Both the declaration and destruction of stockpiles and production facilities and subsequent monitoring of compliance with provisions for non-production of chemical weapons must be verified under adequate international control. Verification measures should include a combination of voluntary confidence-building measures, national verification measures, and agreed international means.

Developing countries have a special interest in ensuring compliance with a treaty banning stockpiles and production of chemical weapons. Since very few developing states have the technology to develop adequate national means of verification, international means are necessary also in order to protect their interest.

Over the past fifteen years scientific understanding of the molecular and cellular processes of life has grown enormously. So far there is no evidence of military exploitation of this knowledge. Should the biological sciences be tapped for military purposes, however, hideous new weapons could emerge. Our well-being and economic and social development could be drastically retarded.

The Commission calls for an international convention which would prohibit any secret development or experimentation in the military applications of molecular biology and its associated disciplines.

2.4 Universal adherence to the Non-Proliferation Treaty

Preventing the spread of nuclear weapons is a critical element in any international effort to halt and reverse the nuclear arms race and ensure the maintenance of international peace and security. Progress in this direction demands obligations and responsibilities on the part of both nuclear-weapon states and non-nuclear-weapon states.

The problem of proliferation has fallen into two sections, popularly termed 'vertical' and 'horizontal' proliferation. Vertical proliferation refers to the growth of the stockpiles of nuclear weapons held by existing nuclear-weapon states. Horizontal proliferation refers to the spreading of nuclear weaponry to new countries. Efforts to stop both kinds of proliferation resulted in the conclusion of the Non-Proliferation Treaty in 1970, which committed non-nuclear-weapon states to refrain from acquiring such weapons and the nuclear-weapon states to halting and reversing their processes of qualitative and quantitative growth of nuclear weapons.

The Non-Proliferation Treaty is the centerpiece of the widespread international interest in maintaining the presumption against proliferation. One hundred and eighteen states are now parties to the treaty. However, France and China, which are nuclear-weapon states, as well as a number of important countries on the threshold of being able to build nuclear weapons, have so far failed to sign and ratify the treaty. *The Commission urges all states to adhere to the Non-Proliferation Treaty.*

Some opponents of the treaty point to its discriminatory nature, accepting nuclear weapons for those five countries which already have them but forbidding others to develop similar capabilities. But, by its very nature, non-proliferation involves a degree of discrimination. The key issue is how this fact of life is handled. The Commission recognizes that the failure of the nuclear-weapon states to make progress towards nuclear disarmament, as promised in Article VI of the Non-Proliferation Treaty, affects the attitudes and commitments of others. The proposals we have made for a complete nuclear test ban, for the reduction and withdrawal of nuclear arms in Europe and in the Soviet and American stockpiles, are a reflection of our concern to strengthen the treaty's appeal. Failure to stop vertical proliferation will compromise the integrity of the Non-Proliferation Treaty.

2.5 Safeguarding the nuclear fuel cycle

International cooperation is needed in order to reduce the danger that the development and application of peaceful uses of nuclear energy may lead to diversion of nuclear materials for military purposes. *Particularly sensitive parts of the nuclear fuel cycle should be placed under international authority. This could include the establishment of international fuel banks, an international plutonium storage scheme, and internationally managed sites for spent fuel storage.* Regional organizations can contribute significantly to such international arrangements, which should be drawn together by the International Atomic Energy Agency through its Committee on Assurance of Supply.

Participants in the 1977-80 International Fuel Cycle Evaluation acknowledged that fuels usable in weapons require special procedures. The Committee on Assurance of Supply of the International Atomic Energy Agency may be developed into a central negotiating and management forum comprising both suppliers and recipient countries. Such cooperation would conform with Article IV of the Non-Proliferation Treaty which underlines the need for equitable cooperation in the use of nuclear energy for peaceful purposes.

2.6 The need to limit conventional arms transfers

The volume of arms transfers has more than doubled during the past decade. Deliveries are now close to $30 billion per annum and orders are substantially higher. More than three quarters of all arms transfers go to the countries of the developing world.

In our view, there is an urgent need for a concerted effort to develop a fair system of guidelines and restraints covering arms exports, based on cooperation among recipient and supplier states.

Supplier states should open talks aimed at establishing criteria by which they could regulate arms transfers on an equitable basis. Restraints need to be defined in terms of quantities and qualities, geography and military circumstances. The guidelines for arms transfer should include such principles as

- No significant increase in the quantity of weapons which are transferred to a region.

- No first introduction of advanced weapon systems into a region which create new or significantly higher levels of combat capability.

- Special restrictions on the transfer of lethal weapons to warring parties, taking into account the inherent right of individual or collective self-defence.

- Adherence to the implementation of UN resolutions and sanctions.

- No transfer of particularly inhumane and indiscriminate weapons.

- Special precautions to be taken when transferring weapons, such as hand-held anti-aircraft weapons, which, if they fell into the hands of individuals or sub-national groups, would be especially dangerous.

The United States and the Soviet Union held Conventional Arms Transfer talks in 1977-80. The Commission endorses the resumption of such talks which should include also France, the United Kingdom, and other major supplier states. Another need is for talks between supplier states and recipients in regions where tensions are particularly severe. There is a need for multilateral restraints.

Recipient states should similarly undertake to develop guidelines and codes of conduct designed to curb the flow of arms and avoid arms races. An important beginning was made by eight Andean states in the Declaration of Ayacucho in 1974 in which they pledged to 'create conditions which permit effective limitation of armaments and put an end to their acquisition for offensive warlike purposes in order to dedicate all possible resources to economic and social development'. Regrettably, the discussion of specific restraints broke down. However, at a meeting in Mexico City in 1978, twenty Latin American and Caribbean states agreed to exchange information on weapon purchases and work towards a regime of restraints on arms transfers.

Recipient states may wish to bar or limit certain types of weapon. They may consider that if those weapons were used in their part of the world they would enhance offensive capacities and introduce incentives for rapid action in a crisis. They may wish, too, to outlaw weapons which are starkly inhumane in their effects. The 'rules of the game' will need to be tailored to the specific circumstances of the area in question. Regional Conferences on Security and Cooperation could discuss general principles. States which are participating in zones of peace or similar groupings could decide on more specific guidelines. The latter would have to be adhered to also by the supplier states.

3 Assuring confidence among states

Adequate verification is an important part of any agreement on arms limitation or reduction. States are loath to enter into such agreements on the basis of good faith alone. The development of the so-called national technical means gave the parties to arms control agreements confidence that they could monitor compliance with the provisions of treaties adequately. Technologies used to observe and monitor military activities have advanced impressively. Military secrecy still exists, however.

Consequently, monitoring compliance with treaty proscriptions remains an issue in negotiations. There should be a close link between the scope and design of treaties and the means prescribed for their verification. There are no all-purpose forms of verification. Requirements have to be determined in each specific instance. Verification requires cooperative arrangements and, in some instances, on-site inspections.

While the purpose of verification is to provide for timely detection of any illegal, surreptitious activity, it could hopefully also lead to improved confidence among treaty parties and promote compliance with treaty norms.

3.1 Confidence-building measures relating to military expenditure, research and development

Satellites can only detect forces in being or in formation. However, it takes from seven to fifteen years for a modern weapon system to move through the various stages of research, development, testing and deployment. States hedge against the possible future results of decisions other states may have made today, assuming the worst about the decisions of the adversary. Confidence building is necessary if the spirals of suspicion and fear are to be broken.

The greater sharing of information about budgetary expenditure, for example, could enhance confidence. A standardized reporting system has been developed and tried out under the auspices of the United Nations. The 35th General Assembly of the United Nations urged all states to report information about their expenditure for military purposes in accordance with the system. *The Commission urges all states to comply with the resolution of the General Assembly.*[43]

In view of the momentum and vested interests which affect the process of military research and development, *the Commission urges the major industrial powers to conduct a dialogue about questions relating to research and development of all types of military forces.* This would provide an opportunity to voice concerns about the implications of actual and possible programmes, so that the response could be taken into account prior to national decisions about procurement and deployment. The danger of unintended destabilization and aggravated competition could thereby be reduced.

Having outlined a programme for arms control and disarmament in relation primarily to the competition and conflicts among the industrialized countries, we focus on the need to promote international security in a global context with emphasis on the developing world.

4 Strengthening the United Nations security system

We are convinced of the need to strengthen the security role of the United Nations. A new conceptual approach must be developed in order to promote common security in the world at large.

4.1 More effective use of the Security Council and the Secretary General

Within the UN, primary responsibility for maintaining inter-

161

national peace and security rests with the Security Council. Regrettably, states have tended only to turn to the Council as a last resort when conflict has already, or is on the verge of breaking out. If they are to be persuaded to shed this attitude, *the Security Council itself must enhance its capacity to preempt conflicts. The permanent members, in particular, should seek to foster a close understanding and collaboration among themselves and encourage a mutually supportive partnership with the Secretary General to facilitate initiatives under Article 99 of the Charter.*

Article 99 specifically authorizes the Secretary General 'to bring to the attention of the Security Council any matter which in his opinion may threaten the maintenance of international peace and security'. *The Security Council should adopt an initiating resolution explicitly calling upon the Secretary General to bring to its immediate attention potential threats to the peace. In addition, we recommend that the Secretary General should report to the Council on a regular basis throughout the year. There should be a special annual 'state of the international community' message to be delivered in person by the Secretary General to a meeting of the Security Council with the Foreign Ministers in attendance.* This message should be delivered at a public session so that all states become aware of the Secretary General's assessment. It should be followed by a private discussion of its implications by the Foreign Ministers of Security Council members. They should attempt to identify specific measures which the Council might take to head off possible conflicts.

To help assert the UN's primacy in international peace and security and to enhance the role of the Security Council we believe that it would be useful for the Council to hold occasional meetings outside UN headquarters. This would provide the opportunity for a more focused discussion and consultation on the problems of a particular region.

4.2 Collective security – a first step

A key proposal in our recommendations is the implementation of a modified version of the UN Charter's concept of collective security. Its basis would be political agreement and partnership between the permanent members of the Security Council and Third World countries. Its scope would be limited to Third World conflicts

162

arising out of border disputes or threats to territorial integrity caused by other factors. Its purpose would be to prevent the conflicts from being settled by armed force, and not to pronounce on the substantive issues in dispute. It would be underpinned by an understanding – 'concordat' – among the permanent members of the Security Council to support collective security action, at least, to the extent possible, of not voting against it. The cooperation of the permanent members of the Security Council is particularly important. Their consent is a prerequisite for the effective functioning of the United Nations in maintaining international peace and security.

As distinct from peacekeeping operations, collective security procedures would have anticipatory, preventive, and enforcement elements. They would all be integrally linked, each reinforcing the other.

At the anticipatory and preventive levels three phases of UN action would be necessary:

(i) On being alerted by at least one of the disputing parties to the danger of a possible conflict, the Secretary General would constitute a *fact-finding mission* to advise him on the situation.

(ii) If circumstances warrant, and with the consent of at least one of the disputing parties, the Secretary General would seek the authorization of the Security Council to send a *military observer team* to the requesting state to assess the situation in military terms and to demonstrate the Council's serious concern.

(iii) In the light of circumstances and the report of the military observers, the Security Council would authorize the induction of an appropriate *UN military force* at the request of one of the disputing states with a view to preventing conflict. This force would be deployed within the likely zone of hostilities, in the territory of the requesting state, thereby providing a visible deterrent to a potential aggressor.

All three phases would be covered by the political concordat among the permanent members of the Security Council whereby they would commit themselves to support particular types of collective security action, and thereby placed on an assured basis.

163

The introduction of substantial UN forces before the outbreak of hostilities would, in most cases, prevent violations of territory from occurring at all. Nevertheless, there could be situations where violation of territory might still take place with an attack so sudden as to preempt the possibility of effective preventive measures. In such circumstances limited enforcement measures would become necessary. The first objective would be to establish a negotiated ceasefire. The Council would call on the warring parties to cease hostilities and notify them of the dispatch of collective security forces to establish and maintain an effective ceasefire. The parties would be asked to cooperate fully in the achievement of this objective, it being clearly understood that UN forces would have the right of self-defence if attacked by either of the two warring parties.

Full-scale collective security enforcement action would, of course, imply restoration of the *status quo ante* through military means. This is the ultimate deterrent enshrined in Chapter VII of the Charter. Although not realizable in the immediate future, it must remain a goal towards which the international community works.

For the present, other means could be used to ensure that aggression does not prevail. The introduction of a ceasefire should be accompanied by an appeal by the Security Council to the aggressor state to withdraw its troops to its original borders. In the event of a refusal to comply, the Council would immediately consider ways of enforcing its will through the other provisions of Chapter VII, including the imposition of mandatory economic sanctions.

4.3 Process of implementation
We identify the following key components for implementing our approach to collective security:

(i) *Third World support*
   The Non-Aligned Movement has long been an advocate of a strengthened UN role in international security. Its support would be critical in facilitating the proposed concordat among the permanent members of the Security Council.

(ii) *A political concordat among the veto powers*
   The scope of this concordat would be limited, in both pro-

cedural and operational terms. The permanent members of the Security Council would be committed to supporting collective security action in the manner described, and, at least to the extent possible, to not vote against it.

(ii) *An operational structure for UN standby forces*
Article 43 envisages agreements between the UN and member governments on the provision of military standby forces. The Military Staff Committee should be reactivated and strengthened for this purpose. Furthermore, the respective roles of the Secretary General and the Military Staff Committee would need to be carefully considered so as to ensure that enforcement action by the UN is not allowed to become, or perceived by Third World countries to be, a vehicle for great power interference. Standby forces should not be recruited exclusively or overwhelmingly from the forces of the permanent members of the Security Council. We consider it particularly important that a greater number of Third World countries should become potential contributors of standby forces. This objective could be accomplished most readily on a regional basis. Where states of the region deem it suitable, regional or sub-regional cooperation for the establishment, equipping and training of standby forces along the lines that have already been successfully developed by the Nordic states should be actively encouraged.

The presence of standby forces in a particular region where it was thought that enforcement action might be required would mean that they could be rapidly deployed to the scene of the conflict, either to be stationed on the border as a deterrent to aggression or to establish a ceasefire as soon as possible after a violation of territory has taken place. In the case of Africa, arrangements establishing standby forces within the region, moreover, would provide the necessary military infrastructure to enable the Organization of African Unity to effectively contribute to peacekeeping operations which it may have itself initiated, even though the necessary funding and specialized technical support might still have to be provided under UN auspices.

Specifically, in connection with the proposal for establishing a UN collective security system, we envisage that regional organizations could play a vital role in alerting the Security Council and the UN Secretary General to the danger of an imminent threat to the peace and in supplementing UN efforts to maintain peace.

4.4 Improved capability for peacekeeping

Since our proposal on collective security will not apply to all conflict situations, there will be continuing need for UN peacekeeping operations. We recommend that a small complement of professional military personnel be included in the staff of the Under-Secretary General for Special Political Affairs who is responsible to the Secretary General for the coordination and management of all peacekeeping operations.

Participation in peacekeeping operations is not compulsory but voluntary and only a small number of countries have responded to the UN's call in the past. *We believe steps should be taken to encourage wider participation in peacekeeping through:*

(a) *A General Assembly resolution requesting states to incorporate training for peacekeeping as part of their armies' basic training course, assisted by a standard training manual issued by the UN Secretariat.*

(b) *A joint undertaking between states with experience in peacekeeping and an appropriate UN agency to assist in the training and equiping of troops from Third World countries.*

(c) *Regional arrangements to promote units for peacekeeping duties on a standby basis.*

(d) *The stockpiling of certain types of equipment and supplies which are always necessary. This would improve the capacity of the UN to undertake peacekeeping operations at short notice. The major powers should be asked to contribute transportation aircraft and special units for logistic and signals support; other states should be asked to earmark units for medical services, including field hospitals. Contribution of special units would also improve capabilities for disaster relief operations.*

The UN also must be prepared to respond to new kinds of challenges to international peace and security. For example, the emergence of extensive piracy in the areas off South East Asia might suggest the creation of a small UN naval patrol force based on the voluntary assignment of naval vessels and crews to UN duty by member states, and the consent of the littoral states.

4.5 An appropriate funding mechanism with built-in automaticity

The UN has experienced great difficulty in eliciting the financial contributions necessary to pay for peacekeeping operations from some member states, including one or two members of the Security Council. We believe that collective security operations and, for other purposes, peacekeeping ones as well, need to be financed through an independent source of revenue.

We underline the importance of adopting a means of automatic financing that spreads the burden widely and fairly throughout the international community. All will benefit, all should contribute.

Pending agreement on automatic funding from an independent source of revenue, we recommend that the General Assembly should agree on a specified percentage surcharge to be added to the assessed contributions of all member countries to the regular budget. These moneys would be placed in a special reserve fund earmarked for implementing all aspects of collective security operations. Current peacekeeping operations, too, would benefit from a similar approach.

5 Regional approaches to security

The Commission's recommendations for strengthening the UN's security system stem from the conviction that there is no alternative to preserving and enhancing the primacy of its role in maintaining international peace. Although Third World countries in recent years have increasingly sought to handle their own conflicts outside the UN, in many of the conflicts neighbouring countries take opposing sides. This demonstrates that a regional approach can often prove inadequate or counter-productive. There are some situations in which a regional forum could provide a more appropriate framework than the UN for arriving at a political settlement, but even in such cases financial and operational limitations at the regional level sometimes work against effective security solutions.

Regional approaches should, therefore, be viewed not as substitutes for UN action, but as a means of complementing and strengthening it. There is a need to develop an operational connection between regional security initiatives and the UN security system. This kind of link, moreover, would be fully in accord with Chapter VIII of the Charter which explicitly anticipates that regions might wish to establish their own arrangements for dealing with matters relating to international peace and security. It makes only two provisos: that these arrangements and bodies must be 'consistent with the purposes and principles of the United Nations', and that 'the Security Council shall at all times be kept fully informed of activities undertaken or in contemplation under regional arrangements or by regional agencies for the maintenance of international peace and security'.

There is a great unexplored potential at the regional level not only to meet and resolve actual conflict situations as they arise, but also to promote a general sense of security through cooperative measures with the aim of facilitating disarmament, encouraging policies of mutual restraint and improving the economic welfare of member states. In making the recommendations set out below, however, the Commission has been conscious that the various regions and sub-regions differ widely in respect both of indigenous rivalries and the degree of involvement by the major powers. We fully appreciate that any initiative for regional cooperation will require regional consensus, but we are convinced that consensus can in turn be consolidated and expanded through cooperation.

5.1 Regional conferences on security and cooperation

The Commission recommends that the countries making up the various regions, and in some instances sub-regions, of the Third World consider the convocation of periodic or ad hoc Regional Conferences on Security and Cooperation similar to the one launched in Helsinki for Europe in 1975. Regional Conferences on Security and Cooperation could add new substance to the concept of common security. The priorities must be developed by the countries concerned and reflect the circumstances in the individual regions both with respect to agenda and participation. The Secretary General of the United Nations should be invited to participate.

It is envisaged that the Regional Conferences could provide an overall framework for cooperation not only on matters directly relating to security, but in the economic, social, and cultural spheres as well.

In the area of security, the Conferences could consider such matters as adoption of codes of conduct and confidence-building measures, establishment of zones of peace and nuclear-weapon-free zones, and agreements on arms limitations and reductions. Subsidiary bodies could be set up to deal with aspects of implementing the Conferences' decisions or to carry out any further studies that might be required. Depending on the character of their membership, Regional Conferences might consider it useful, for instance, to establish a Boundaries Commission to investigate and make recommendations on solutions for border disputes or a similar body to look into difficulties arising from the demarcation of territorial waters and exclusive economic zones. Regional study institutes could be created to analyse security issues of direct relevance to the particular region and to formulate recommendations for the consideration of the Conference; such institutes should be funded by governments and possibly receive a financial input from the UN as well, but should be allowed to operate independently of government direction.

The Regional Conferences would also be the appropriate bodies for launching any regional peacekeeping or peacemaking initiative to meet a given crisis situation. It would, however, be essential for them to keep the Security Council fully informed about any specific security arrangements contemplated. We further recommend that general working procedures for tying regional security arrangements into the UN security system should be formulated. These should preferably be established soon after the Regional Conference is constituted so as to create a standby operational framework for activating cooperation with the UN to cope with conflict situations when it is needed.

In our opinion, the concept of regional security will be unlikely to take root unless it is sustained by programmes for economic cooperation to encourage countries to see themselves as having a national stake in actively working to achieve regional harmony. An important focus of the Regional Conferences must therefore be the establishment of joint projects that are designed to benefit all participating states. The UN's regional economic commissions could have an important part to play in this connection – the Economic Commission for Europe, for example, has performed a valuable function in assisting the development of the Conference on Security and Cooperation in Europe. Involvement of these Commissions would moreover ensure a UN contribution of funds and technical assistance for security-building through economic cooperation. This would provide an effective infrastructure for the link between regional security initiatives and the UN security system.

The Regional Conferences could also consider schemes for regional cooperation on the peaceful exploitation of nuclear energy in a manner which would strengthen an equitable non-proliferation regime. Regional cooperation could comprise regional fuel banks, plutonium storage schemes and arrangements for spent fuel management. It could provide structure and substance to general international projects which should be drawn together by the International Atomic Energy Agency.

5.2 Zones of peace
The creation of zones of peace has been proposed most notably for the Indian Ocean and South East Asian areas.* Within the zone, peace should be maintained by the countries themselves through the peaceful resolution of disputes in a context of political and economic cooperation, as well as mutual military restraint. An essential factor in ensuring its viability, however, is agreement by outside powers to respect its purposes and specific provisions.

Zones of peace would be a flexible mechanism for developing cooperation at the sub-regional level, while the proposed Regional Conferences on Security and Cooperation could provide a general framework for considering objectives and experiences of the

---

*See *Final Document of the Tenth Special Session of the General Assembly*, New York, United Nations, 1972, A/RES/S-1012 pp. 14–15; and *Study on All the Aspects of Regional Disarmament*, New York, United Nations, 1981, A/35/416 pp. 15–19.

different zones within their region and for establishing links between them. States within the zones could cooperate on developing a code of conduct and confidence-building measures as well as on an agreement to limit arms competition. Some important suggestions along these lines were put forward by the President of Mexico in February 1982 as part of a proposal to further a relaxation of tensions in Central America. The main elements encompass renunciation of all threats or use of force, balanced reduction of military troops in the area, and a system of non-aggression pacts.

It is important to note that the Kuala Lumpur Declaration of 1971 on the establishment of South East Asia as a Zone of Peace, Freedom and Neutrality was issued by a grouping of countries which had already put significant emphasis on economic, social and cultural cooperation and had formed themselves into the Association of South East Asian Nations to further this objective. Similarly, the Economic Community of West African States started its existence in 1975 as a purely economic grouping and in 1981 its sixteen West African member states adopted a Protocol on Mutual Assistance in Defence Matters. The Gulf Cooperation Council, established in 1981 with the ultimate aim of achieving unity of their six member countries, has likewise stressed the need to build 'coordination, integration and cooperation in all fields'.

The Commission considers that the concept of zones of peace could be an important contribution to the maintenance of international peace and security. Political difficulties that might seem to militate against is realization in the immediate future should not, in our view, inhibit groups of countries from continuing their work towards the establishment of such zones as a long-term objective.

5.3 Nuclear-weapon-free zones

The Commission believes that the establishment of nuclear-weapon-free zones on the basis of arrangements freely arrived at among the states of the region or sub-region concerned, constitutes an important step towards non-proliferation, common security and disarmament. They could provide mutual reassurance to states preferring not to acquire or allow deployment of nuclear weapons as long as neighbouring states exercise similar restraint. This would improve the chances for the region not to become enveloped in the

171

competition of the nuclear-weapon states. The nuclear-weapon states would have to undertake a binding commitment to respect the status of the zone, and not to use or threaten to use nuclear weapons against the states of the zone.

The Treaty of Tlatelolco, prohibiting nuclear weapons in Latin America, is a path-breaking regional arrangement in this field. A party to it is not bound, though, until all the signatories have completed ratification, unless it waives this condition. Brazil and Chile have not done so. At present the treaty is in force for twenty-two Latin American states. Argentina has signed but not ratified the treaty. Cuba has neither signed nor ratified. The Commission strongly urges all states concerned to adopt all relevant measures to ensure the full application of the treaty.

Proposals for creating nuclear-weapon-free zones in Africa, the South Pacific, South Asia and the Middle East have been put forward in the United Nations and have received support in the General Assembly. The process of establishing nuclear-weapon-free zones in different parts of the world should be encouraged with the ultimate objective of achieving a world entirely free of nuclear weapons.

Should it prove impossible to agree on legally defined nuclear-weapon-free zones, states could, as an interim measure, pledge themselves not to become the first to introduce nuclear weapons in the region. The nuclear-weapon states would have to guarantee the countries concerned that they would not be threatened or attacked with such weapons.

6 Economic security

The present condition of the world economy threatens the security of every country. *The Commission believes that just as countries cannot achieve security at each other's expense, so too they cannot achieve security through military strength alone.* Common security requires that people live in dignity and peace, that they have enough to eat and are able to find work and live in a world without poverty and destitution.

6.1 The costs of military spending
Military competition reduces both military and economic security.

172

Military spending is part of the problem, not part of the solution. The human cost of military effort has long been apparent in a world where more than 1,000 million men, women and children have no chance to learn to read and write, and more than 600 million are hungry or starving.

But the economic problems of the 1970s and early 1980s make the waste of human effort even more intolerable. The presumed economic benefits of military spending are a dangerous illusion. Increased military spending would make our economic problems worse, not better. Military expenditure is likely to create less employment than other forms of public expenditure, with greater risks for inflation and for future economic growth. These dangers are exacerbated by the peculiar character of the modern military effort, with its increasing emphasis in both developed and developing countries alike on expensive, technologically sophisticated armaments. All but a very few countries now face the most troubling choices in deciding how to spend their limited government revenues – on health programmes or on improving the lives of old people, on unemployment benefits or on investment in economic growth and development, on education or on foreign aid. The costs of military spending must be counted in terms of these other opportunities forgone.

6.2 Disarmament and development

The link between disarmament and development, in the new economic context of the 1980s, is close and compelling. The 'crisis' in the world economy described by the Brandt Commission in 1980 has become even more serious. The military tensions analysed in the present report have been a major contributory factor in making this crisis worse. But the process of building common security could help to resolve it. In the first place, for several developing countries, military expenditure, particularly on sophisticated imported weapons, threatens the economic development which is the only basis for lasting security. In the second place, revenues now used on the military could constitute a major source for increasing development assistance by developed and capital-surplus countries. Some governments argue that they cannot increase or even maintain their foreign aid because of competing domestic claims on government resources. These claims are real and urgent. But even a tiny share of the expenditure currently going to military purposes – about $650 billion a year – would go a long way towards resolving the Third World's pressing needs. Third, reductions in military spending would increase the prospects for resumed growth in the world economy, and thus for worldwide economic security. Developing countries need to import the goods and services that developed countries need to export. Resources saved from the military could finance this expansion. We share the view that such economic recovery is an essential investment in future security.

Limiting military competition would have immense benefits for the security of all countries; it would have economic benefits as well. Reductions in military spending will provide resources to reduce poverty and increase social wellbeing even in the richest military powers. They should also provide resources for development.

Schemes for linking disarmament and development will be different in different countries and regions. In countries with large military expenditures, they should take the form of releasing resources from defence budgets for foreign development assistance. The main military powers spend from four to over one hundred times as much on defence as on foreign economic aid. A ten per cent cut in procurement by the nuclear powers alone would be more than enough to double total foreign aid and other financial flows to the thirty-one least-developed countries. Such rather mechanical calculations would probably not lead to appropriate targets, although there is certainly need for international cooperation in discussing the various possibilities for verifying the switching of resources from the military to development. It might be possible, instead, to devise targets described in physical terms; countries might announce that they would use funds from their defence budget to build a fertilizer factory, for example, or to contribute the services of a hundred paramedical workers. It is up to the imagination of people in each country to find ways to participate in such 'peace competition'.

6.3 Regional conferences on disarmament and economic security

It is essential that people and governments in all regions should participate in finding new resources for development. The Commission urges that one of the first topics for the Regional

Conferences described in recommendation 5.1, including the Conference on Security and Cooperation in Europe, should be disarmament and economic security. *Countries should consider convening a high-level conference to discuss common problems of economic security, and their common interest in reducing the regional costs of military spending.* Such a conference could provide an opportunity to inform people and governments about the economic costs of military competition; to initiate cooperation in providing information and analysis about military spending; to initiate common efforts to achieve more security at less cost.

The Commission urges that the Regional Conferences launch major campaigns to increase public awareness of the dangers of military competition, including the dangers for economic security. Such campaigns should be an initial step in a continuing long-term public-education effort. Their cost could be met with a small fraction of one per cent of regional military expenditure. The United Nations should coordinate the efforts of regional conferences and participate actively in the information campaigns.

The Commission finds it unacceptable that a substantial share of the world's scientific potential be devoted to ever more refined forms of destruction, while our countries urgently need research into preventing and curing disease, into new methods of food production, into alleviating the problems of old people, and into preserving the physical environment. The Regional Conferences should consider ways of converting to civilian uses the scientific and technical resources now consumed for military purposes: from research and development workers and facilities in developed and certain developing countries to technicians with scarce industrial skills throughout the world. The real social costs of devoting resources to military spending vary greatly in different regions, and should accordingly be discussed at a regional level. *The Regional Conferences should propose detailed programmes to use military skills for urgent civilian needs in the particular region. Such schemes should include national plans to convert specific military facilities - research establishments or other military installations - to civilian purposes.*

6.4 Common security and common prosperity

We share the conviction of the Brandt Commission that the South

175

and the North, the East and the West have 'mutual interests' in economic progress. No country can resolve its problems alone. A reduction in the present high levels of military spending would therefore be in the economic interests of all countries, even those who spend relatively little on their own military efforts.

The principle of common security asserts that countries can only find security in cooperation with their competitors, not against them.

No country can hope to win military advantage by out-running its competitor in an economically costly arms race. All countries are hurt by the economic difficulties of the major economies. Common security is not only a matter of freedom from military fear. Its objective is not only to avoid being killed in a nuclear apocalypse, or in a border dispute, or by a machine gun in one's own village. Its objective, in the end, is to live a better life: in common security and common prosperity.

Annexe One:
A programme of action

The proposals we have presented in this report are based on the principle of common security. We are convinced that there would be no victors in nuclear war and that the idea of fighting a limited nuclear war is dangerous. In the nuclear age, states cannot achieve security through competition in arms. They must cooperate to attain the limitation, reduction and eventual abolition of arms. Furthermore, they must develop procedures to resolve conflicts peacefully and stress those modes of national behaviour which are consistent with the achievement of common security through cooperative efforts.

Elements of a programme for arms limitation and disarmament

We believe that the ultimate goal must be general and complete disarmament. Consistent with that aim we have identified such long-term objectives as sharp reductions in strategic nuclear arms through progressive stages of small, secure, retaliatory forces. Furthermore, we have endorsed the long-term objective of agreements on substantial conventional disarmament in Europe and the eventual elimination of all nuclear weapons that threaten Europe.

There is an immediate need to initiate a downward turn in the arms spiral. We have, therefore, proposed a set of short- and medium-term measures. The short-term measures could, and should, be implemented within the next two years; the medium-term measures within the next five years. We recognize that what we have proposed is an ambitious programme. It goes well beyond that which present governments seem willing to attempt. However, we are convinced that governments must raise their sights and commit

177

themselves to a concentrated effort to turn the tide and inaugurate an era of common security. What we propose are realistic and attainable objectives.

Short-term measures
- Agreements on any necessary clarifications or adjustments of the 1979 SALT II Treaty.
- Preservation of the Anti-Ballistic Missile Treaty of 1972.
- Conclusion of a first phase agreement on mutual force reductions in Central Europe by a Foreign Ministers' meeting.
- Opening of talks on the establishment of a battlefield-nuclear-weapon-free zone in Central Europe.
- Non-deployment of 'mini-nukes' and enhanced radiation (neutron) weapons in Europe.
- Soviet–American agreement on rough parity in intermediate-(medium-) range nuclear forces at a level which means that NATO will forgo the introduction of a new generation of intermediate- (medium-) range nuclear missiles in Europe.
- Soviet–American agreement on banning the forward deployment of new short-range nuclear weapon systems which could threaten the same European targets which are threatened by intermediate-range nuclear systems.
- Agreement on the establishment of a chemical-weapon-free zone in Europe.
- Agreement to convene a conference on confidence- and security-building measures and disarmament in Europe.
- Agreement on a comprehensive nuclear test ban.
- Agreement on a ban on anti-satellite weapon tests and the dismantling of existing systems.
- Opening of negotiations on a ban on the deployment of anti-satellite weapons.
- Resumption of Soviet–American talks on a chemical weapons disarmament treaty.
- Agreement on consultative procedures for the resolution of problems arising under the 1925 Geneva Protocol prohibiting the use of chemical weapons and the 1975 Biological Warfare Convention.
- Broader adherence to the Non-Proliferation Treaty.
- Opening of talks between supplier states and recipient states and

178

among supplier states on guidelines for regulating conventional arms transfers.

- Broad compliance with the General Assembly resolution on reporting military expenditures to the United Nations in accordance with a standardized reporting system.
- Regional conferences on security and cooperation should discuss economic security and reduction of the region-wide costs of military spending.
- Launch of a major campaign to increase public awareness of the dangers of military competition, including dangers for economic security.
- Devising specific national plans for releasing resources from defence budgets for foreign development assistance.

Medium-term measures
- Soviet–American agreement on substantial additional reductions in strategic offensive forces and on qualitative limitation relating to such forces.
- Agreement on equal ceilings for NATO and the Warsaw Pact in respect of conventional forces in Central Europe at reduced levels.
- In the context of parity in conventional forces, establishment of a battlefield-nuclear-weapon-free zone in Europe, starting with Central Europe and extending ultimately from the northern to the southern flanks of the two alliances.
- Agreement on substantial reductions in battlefield nuclear weapons in Europe.
- Opening of negotiations about the reduction of the remaining nuclear weapons in Europe, including dual-capable aircraft.
- Agreement on a 'second generation' of confidence- and security-building measures in Europe.
- Opening of negotiations for disarmament throughout Europe.
- Agreement on a total ban on the deployment of anti-satellite weapons.
- Conclusion of a comprehensive chemical weapons disarmament treaty banning the production and stockpiling of all such weapons and the destruction of existing stocks and production facilities.
- International convention prohibiting any secret development or

experimentation in the military applications of molecular biology and its associated disciplines.

- Universal adherence to the Non-Proliferation Treaty.
- Agreements on the internationalization of particularly sensitive parts of the nuclear fuel cycle.
- Agreements on supplier- and recipient-state guidelines for conventional arms transfers.
- Universal compliance with the General Assembly resolution on reporting military expenditure to the United Nations in accordance with a standardized reporting system.
- Substantial reduction in military spending in developed and developing countries, releasing resources for national needs and development assistance.
- Conversion of a large proportion of military, scientific and technological efforts to civilian purposes.

With regard to international security in the Third World we have outlined certain procedures which should be developed and refined, rather than proposed specific measures. Implementation should take place through the decade of the 1980s with the aim of promoting United Nations procedures and regional cooperative arrangements which are more suited to coping with the challenges in the post-colonial world order than present procedures.

Procedures for strengthening the United Nations
In order to enhance the Security Council's capacity to preempt conflicts:

- The Secretary General should report to the Security Council on a regular basis throughout the year, and in addition present an annual 'state of the international community' message to the Security Council at the Foreign Minister level.
- The Security Council should meet from time to time outside the UN headquarters.
- Implementation of a first step towards collective security in Third World conflicts arising out of border disputes, including procedures for fact finding, military observation and introduction of UN forces. It should be based on Third World support, a political 'concordat' among the veto-powers, and the availability of standby forces.

- Creation of improved capabilities for UN peacekeeping through the adoption of standard training manuals; assistance to Third World countries in training and equipment; regional arrangements for standby forces; stockpiling of equipment and earmaking of special units.
- Agreement on appropriate funding mechanisms for peace-keeping and collective security operations with built-in automaticity.

Regional approaches to security
- Convocation of Regional Conferences on Security and Cooperation.
- Establishment of zones of peace.
- Establishment of nuclear-weapon-free zones.

Annexe Two:
Comment by Egon Bahr
to page 146

The Commission discussed, with the support of some members, my additional proposal to reduce the nuclear threat in Europe. The proposal, which starts from the principle of common security, has three elements:

1 All nuclear weapons should be withdrawn from European states which do not themselves possess nuclear weapons.
2 In the area of conventional forces, an approximate balance should be attained between NATO and the Warsaw Pact.
3 Both alliance systems, with their obligations and guarantees, should remain unaltered.

1 Europe would not thereby become a nuclear-weapon-free zone. Nuclear weapons would remain in the hands of the four states which already possess them. There would, however, be a zone free of nuclear weapons, threatened by or under the protection of the nuclear powers in possession of weapons of differing range which can be brought into use in the event of a conflict. But the danger of escalation would be reduced; since if there are no dangerous targets the use of dangerous weapons will become unnecessary. The entire discussion on whether wars can be limited and on lowering the nuclear threshold would become pointless.

2 A nuclear-weapon-free zone in Europe demands a balance of conventional forces, i.e. the elimination of that superiority in conventional arms against which nuclear weapons are currently held to be indispensable. Without the readiness to achieve a balance of conventional forces, there is no realistic prospect of a nuclear-weapon-free zone in Europe, since neither side can be permitted to have the advantage over the other.

3 The alliances remain indispensable in the interest of stability and

182

security. Their principle, that the violation of the frontier of one partner is to be considered as an attack on the security of all the others, also corresponds to the idea of common security. Common security can be achieved only with the alliances, and with their leading powers, certainly not against or without them.

The suggested arrangement has the advantage of being simple and unambiguous. It would alter the political atmosphere in the world for the better, and significantly reduce the danger of a collision course. Even the intention of negotiating such an agreement would provide the world with new hope.

Annexe Three:
The Commission and its work

The Independent Commission on Disarmament and Security Issues was launched in Vienna, Austria, on 13 September 1980, after a two-day meeting where the chairman and some members discussed the task for the Commission, its terms of reference and work programme. Preparatory meetings had been held from early 1980.

Much of the structure of the work of the Commission was borrowed from the Brandt Commission (the Independent Commission on International Development Issues under the chairmanship of former West German Chancellor Willy Brandt). In its terms of reference, the Commission stated its intention to seek to complete the Brandt Commission's overview of global problems. Three of the members of ICDSI were also members of the Brandt Commission (Mr Palme, Mr Mori, and Mr Ramphal).

The Commission stated that it intended to publish a report with its recommendations in 1982. In addition to that, the Commission decided to express its opinion on current disarmament and security issues by making public statements during the process of its work. This procedure was followed at almost all meetings. The Commission stressed the need to inform public opinion and decided to keep in close contact with non-governmental organizations.

The Commissioners

The members of the Commission were invited by the chairman to serve in a private capacity, and not under instruction from their respective governments.

Chairman
Olof Palme, Sweden. Member of the Swedish Parliament, former Prime Minister of Sweden, Chairman of the Swedish Social Democratic Party.

Members
Giorgi Arbatov, USSR. Full member of the Central Committee of the Communist Party of the Soviet Union, Deputy of the Supreme Soviet, Academician and Director of the Institute of the USA and Canada, Academy of Sciences of the USSR.

Egon Bahr, Federal Republic of Germany. Member of the German Parliament, Chairman of the Bundestag Subcommittee on Disarmament and Arms Control, former Minister for Economic Cooperation.

Gro Harlem Brundtland, Norway. Member of the Norwegian Parliament, former Prime Minister of Norway, Chairman of the Norwegian Labour Party.

Jozef Cyrankiewicz, Poland. Former Prime Minister of Poland, former President of the Council of State.

Jean-Marie Daillet, France. Member of the French Parliament, Vice Chairman of the Parliament's Defence Committee, Chairman of the UDF Defence Committee. (Suspended his participation in Jan. 1982.)

Robert A. D. Ford, Canada. Ambassador, Special Adviser on East–West relations to the Government of Canada, former Ambassador to Colombia, Yugoslavia, Egypt, and the USSR.

Alfonso Garcia-Robles, Mexico. Ambassador, Chairman of the Mexican Delegation to the Committee on Disarmament since 1967, former Foreign Minister of Mexico.

Haruki Mori, Japan. Former Ambassador to the United Kingdom and to the OECD, former Vice Minister in the Ministry of Foreign Affairs.

C. B. Muthamma, India. Ambassador of India to the Netherlands, former Ambassador to Ghana and Hungary.

Olusegun Obasanjo, Nigeria. General, Member of the Council of State and Distinguished Fellow of the University of Ibadan, former Head of State.

David Owen, United Kingdom. Member of the British Parliament, former Secretary of State for Foreign and Commonwealth Affairs.

Shridath Ramphal, Guyana. Secretary General of the Commonwealth, former Foreign Minister of Guyana.

Salim Salim, Tanzania. Minister of Foreign Affairs of Tanzania.

Soedjatmoko, Indonesia. Rector of the UN University in Tokyo, former Ambassador of Indonesia to the USA.

Joop den Uyl, Netherlands, Member of the Dutch Parliament, Deputy Prime Minister and former Prime Minister, Leader of the Dutch Labour Party.

Cyrus Vance, USA. Former Secretary of State of the United States of America.

185

Scientific advisers
James F. Leonard, USA. Former Deputy Representative of the US to the United Nations, former US Representative to the Geneva Disarmament Committee. James F. Leonard succeeded Leslie H. Gelb, USA, who served as adviser from September 1980 to May 1981.

Mikhail Milstein, USSR. Head of Department at the Institute of the USA and Canada, Academy of Sciences of the USSR. Lieutenant General, retired.

Scientific consultant
Johan Jørgen Holst, Norway. Director of the Norwegian Institute of International Affairs, former State Secretary for Foreign Affairs and for Defence.

Experts
Barry M. Blechman, USA.
Emma Rothschild, UK.
Raimo Väyrynen, Finland.

Coordinator for non-governmental organizations
James George, Canada.

Executive secretary
Anders Ferm, Sweden.

Secretariat
The Chancellor of Austria, Bruno Kreisky invited the Commission to establish its secretariat in Vienna. After negotiations with the Austrian authorities an office was opened in Vienna in late 1980, which was headed by the Executive Secretary. Other members of the secretariat: John Edwards (research secretary), Jagge Andersen (administrative officer), Jonathan Power (editorial adviser), Antoinette Bolza (secretary), Margherita Steinhart (secretary), Maggie Smart (secretary), and Ann-Marie Willsson (secretary).

Connected with the secretariat for various duties has also been Hans Dahlgren (press officer and assistant to the Chairman).

The Commission also received research assistance from: Rebecca Blank, Hilary Bok, Francis J. Connelly, Emine Isvan, and Robert Powell.

Drafts for the final report were prepared by Mr Blechman, Mr Holst and

Miss Rothschild (Economics) and discussed in a panel, consisting of the advisers, consultant, experts, members of the secretariat and chaired by the Executive Secretary. The final content of the report, of course, remains the responsibility of the Commissioners.

Terms of reference

The following terms of reference were adopted:

The Independent Commission on Disarmament and Security Issues has been established against the background of more than three decades of striving for arms control and disarmament. The record is, with some exceptions, tragically disappointing. While mankind has been spared the ultimate horrors of nuclear war, wars continue unabated, international tensions grow, and world expenditure on armaments increases.

The Independent Commission on International Development Issues under the chairmanship of Willy Brandt which completed its report in December 1979 dealt with global issues that would constitute threats to peace in the 1980s, but concentrated its work on economic matters. The new Commission now created will seek to complete that broad overview of global issues by concentrating on security and disarmament measures that can contribute to peace in the 1980s and beyond. The Commission will seek to identify desirable and achievable directions for disarmament and arms control within a comprehensive framework for ensuring national and international security.

The Commission proceeds from the assumption that prospects for real world peace depend to a large extent upon concrete measures and early movement towards not only international economic and social justice but also political and military security. The Commission believes that disarmament and arms control can provide major contributions to international economic development and national security.

The Commission has three goals. First, the long-term goal of helping to chart a course for substantive agreement and actual measures of disarmament with particular regard to the Second United Nations Special Session on Disarmament, to be held in May 1982. Second, the short-term goals of reporting and commenting on current disarmament and security questions with a view to focusing national and international attention on current opportunities for promoting peace through arms limitation. Third, the vitally necessary goal of helping to stimulate an informed public debate on these issues.

To these ends, the Commission will develop a work programme geared to understanding why past efforts of disarmament worked or failed; how progress in current issues of security and arms control could be stimulated; and to proposing longer-term measures of disarmament and arms control that could be usefully pursued at the next UN Special Session on Disarmament.

Meetings

The first meeting was held in Vienna, Austria, on 11–12 September 1980. This meeting discussed the composition of the Commission, the terms of reference and the work programme, as well as financial and organizational matters.

The second meeting took place in Vienna on 13–14 December 1980. The Commission met with Austrian Chancellor Bruno Kreisky and other high Austrian officials. At this meeting, the Commission's terms of reference were adopted. The second meeting discussed the work programme in detail, and decided on studies to be made. The Commission decided how to organize its work including how to keep in contact with the non-governmental organizations.

Also the third meeting was held in Vienna, on 7–8 February 1981. The meeting discussed the SALT process and issued a paper with the title 'The SALT Process: The Global Stakes'. The third meeting also discussed the Vienna Force Reductions Negotiations, after introductions by representatives from the two sides at these talks, Ambassador E. Jung from the Federal Republic of Germany and Ambassador T. Strulak from Poland. Finally, this meeting also dealt with the medical effects of a nuclear exchange. A report on this subject was given to the Commission by Dr Howard Hiatt, Dean of the School of Public Health of Harvard University.

The fourth meeting was held in Geneva, Switzerland, on 25–26 April 1981. The first subject discussed was the Long Range Theatre Nuclear Forces, after an introduction by P. Lellouche from the French Institute for Foreign Relations (IFRI) and M. Milstein. The Commission issued a statement on this subject. Other items discussed included the Comprehensive Test Ban Treaty, where the Commission heard statements by the Soviet and United Kingdom ambassadors to the CD in Geneva, Ambassador Issraelean and Ambassador Summerhayes. Lawrence Freedman and John Simpson (United Kingdom) introduced a paper on this subject. Finally, the meeting dealt with research and development in the military field and new military technology. The Commission heard Bertrand Goldschmidt, France, tell about how the French decision to acquire a nuclear bomb was taken. The subject was also introduced by Bhupendra Jasani (India) and Robert Hunter (USA) who had written papers for the Commission.

The fifth meeting took place in Moscow upon the invitation of the Soviet government, on 12–14 June 1981. The Chairman of the Commision met with the General Secretary of the Communist Party, President Leonid Brezhnev for discussions, and members of the Commission had high-level contacts with Soviet officials. The first subject on the agenda for the meeting was ballistic missile defence systems and the ABM Treaty, and it was introduced by Jack Ruina from the Massachusetts Institute of Technology and by Mikhail Milstein, one of the Commission's scientific advisers. The second subject was the problems of verification of arms control agreements. This was introduced by Barry M. Blechman from the Carnegie Endowment (USA) and by Andrzej Karkoszka from the Polish Institute of International Relations in Warsaw. During the plenary meeting, the Commission had the opportunity to discuss disarmament and security issues with representatives of the Soviet government, First Deputy Foreign Minister G. Kornienko and First Deputy Chief of General Staff, General S. Akhrameev. Furthermore, the Commission had an opportunity to continue its discussion of medical effects of a nuclear war, this time after an introduction by Professor E. Chazov (USSR). At the end of the meeting, the Commission adopted a statement, urging the Soviet Union and the United States to preserve the ABM Treaty.

On 13–18 September 1981, the sixth meeting was held in Mexico City, upon the invitation of the Mexican government. The Chairman met with Mexican President Lopez Portillo, and the Commission was received by Foreign Minister Mr Jorge Castaneda. This was the longest of the Commission's meetings, and it covered many subjects: Security Issues in the Third World (introduction by Swadesh Rana from India), Conventional Arms Transfers (introduced by Barry M. Blechman), Nuclear Proliferation (introduced by P. Lellouche), Nuclear-Weapon-Free Zones (introduced by Raimo Väyrynen from Finland), Armament and Economics (introductory remarks by Wassily Leontief, USA), and Military Doctrines (introduced by R. Hunter and M. Milstein). A statement about nuclear-weapon-free zones and arms transfers was adopted by the Commission. At this meeting the Commission started to discuss drafts for its final report.

In August the Chairman met with French President François Mitterrand and Prime Minister Pierre Mauroy to inform them about the Commission. President Mitterrand invited the Commission to hold its seventh meeting in Paris, France, on 23–25 October 1981 which dealt primarily with economic aspects of military spending. Inga Thorsson presented the report of a UN group of experts on the subject of disarmament and development. A statement by the US Under-Secretary of State for European Affairs, Lawrence Eagleburger, about United States arms control policy was read to the Commission by the US Chargé d'affaires in Paris, Mr Christian Chapman. Emma Rothschild and Lester Thurow of the Massachusetts Institute of Technology introduced a discussion about armaments and economics.

The eight meeting was held in Tokyo on 4–6 December 1981, upon the invitation of a number of Japanese organizations. The Chairman met Prime

Minister Suzuki, Foreign Minister Sakurauchi, and other politicians from Japan and the region. The subjects discussed at the Tokyo meeting included European security problems, possible ways to enhance security in the Third World, and the economic effects of military spending. A press statement was adopted at the end of the meeting. After this meeting, several of the members of the Commission joined Asian politicians, scientists, and other experts in a workshop on disarmament and security issues, with one day's session in Tokyo and another in Hiroshima. This workshop dealt with questions of security in the Asian region. In Hiroshima, the workshop discussed effects of atomic bombings with experts, representatives of Hiroshima and Nagasaki and survivors from the bombings in 1945, and also visited the Memorial Museum.

On 22–24 January 1982, the ninth meeting took place in Schloss Gymnich, outside Bonn, upon the invitation of the government of the Federal Republic of Germany. One subject on the agenda here was the question of chemical weapons, which was discussed after an introduction by Julian Perry Robinson of Sussex University (United Kingdom). Members of the Commission met privately with members of the Federal Government.

The tenth meeting was held on 19–21 February 1982, in Mount Kisco, New York. United Nations Under-Secretary General for Special Political Affairs Brian Urquhart was invited to this meeting to talk about peace-keeping operations. Eugene Rostow, head of the US Arms Control and Disarmament Agency, gave a presentation of the US administration's view on the questions of disarmament and security. Immediately before the meeting the Chairman met with the Secretary General of the United Nations, Senor Javier Perez de Cuellar. At the end of the meeting the Chairman and some members participated in a meeting in Boston with US scientists.

For its eleventh meeting, the Commission was invited by the British government to Ditchley Park outside Oxford, on 19–22 March 1982.

The twelfth meeting was held in Stockholm on 23–25 April 1982, upon the invitation of the Swedish government. Both these meetings dealt exclusively with the final report which was adopted in Stockholm on 25 April 1982.

Papers discussed by the Commission

Instead of establishing a large secretariat with experts in many fields, the Commission decided to ask outside experts from several countries to write papers on the subjects of study and in many cases to introduce these papers at the Commission's meetings. Also members submitted papers for discussion. The papers include:

Howard Hiatt: Medical Effects of a Nuclear Exchange.

Barry M. Blechman: If SALT Fails.

Pierre Lellouche: LRTNF in Europe: Prospects for Meaningful Negotiations.

Soviet expert: About Nuclear Missile Weapons in Europe.

Bhupendra Jasani: Technological Development of Strategic Nuclear Weapons – Towards a First Strike Capability.

John Edwards: Vienna Negotiations on Force Reductions.

Lawrence Freedman and John Simpson: The Comprehensive Test Ban.

Robert E. Hunter: Military Technology in the 1980s.

Soviet expert: The Comprehensive Test Ban.

Barry M. Blechman: Verifying Arms Control Agreements.

Cai Meng-Sun: Views on a Future World War and the Nuclear Arms Race.

Ron Huisken: Armaments and Development.

Andrzej Karkoszka: The Problems of Verification on Arms Limitation Agreements.

Jack Ruina: ABM – New Technology and New Proposals.

William Miller: Review of the Anti-Ballistic-Missile Treaty.

Anthony Lake: Concepts of Security in the 1980s.

Soviet expert: About ABM Defence.

Alfonso Garcia-Robles: The Latin America Nuclear-Weapon-Free Zone.

Swadesh Rana: Security Issues in the Third World – A Strategic Perspective.

Andrzej Karkoszka: Modern Conventional Weapons and some of their Implications for Disarmament and International Security.

Jaako Kalela and Raimo Väyrynen: Nuclear-Weapon-Free Zones New Opportunities in the 1980s?

Robert E. Hunter: Dilemmas of Nuclear Doctrine.

Pierre Lellouche: Non-Proliferation in the 1980s – Guidelines for International Cooperation.

Peter Wallensteen: Patterns of Armed Conflict Since 1945 – An Overview and some Implications.

Leslie H. Gelb: Restraints on International Arms Trade.

Barry M. Blechman: If Efforts to Control Arms Fail.

Soviet expert: About Military Doctrines.

J. P. Perry Robinson: Chemical, Biological and Radiological Warfare; Futures from the Past.

Carol Lancaster and Anthony Lake: Trends in LDC Military Expenditures.

Soviet expert: Economic Aspects of the Arms Race.

Lawrence Freedman and James Schear: International Verification Arrangements.

Lance Taylor: Military Economics in the Third World.

Lester Thurow: The Economics of Rising American Armament Expenditures.

Emma Rothschild: Military Expenditure and Economic Structure.

Egon Bahr: Common Security.

Simon Lunn: Limited Nuclear War.

Lance Taylor: International Adjustment to the Oil Shocks and the Arms Trade.

Johan Jørgen Holst: Security in Europe and Nuclear Weapons – The Need to Turn the Tide.

Bhupendra Jasani and Andrzej Karkoszka: International Verification of Arms Control Agreements.

Persio Arida: Do Unilateral Increases in Military Spending Improve Military Security?

Soviet expert: The Prohibition of Chemical Weapons.

Hiroshima and Nagasaki survivors: Statements from surviving victims of the nuclear attacks on Hiroshima and Nagasaki.

Jack Ruina: Nuclear Testing Limits and Weapons Development.

Acknowledgements

The Commission has received support and advice from many different groups and individuals. Ideas and encouragement have come from political leaders, national and international organizations, religious groups and trade unions, as well as other non-governmental organizations, research institutes, universities. In addition, many concerned citizens have contacted the Commission and its members with valuable suggestions and proposals. The Commission wishes to express its sincere gratitude to all of these.

Financial contributions

The governments of Austria, Canada, Denmark, Finland, Japan, Mexico, Nigeria, Norway, Saudi Arabia, and Sweden have all made untied financial contributions to the work of the Commission. So has the Japanese Shipbuilding Foundation and other private sources. The Soviet government paid for travel to and all local costs at the meeting in Moscow, while a group of Japanese organizations covered travel costs plus all local expenses for the meeting in Tokyo and Hiroshima. Local costs for five Commission meetings were met by the governments of Mexico, France, the Federal Republic of Germany, the United Kingdom, and Sweden. Furthermore, the Nigerian government has offered to host a follow-up meeting later in 1982.

Auditing of ICDSI's accounts was carried out by Dr jur. Peter Wolf in Vienna, Austria.

Follow-up

The Commission's secretariat in Vienna will be closed from 31 July 1982. After that date mail and inquiries can be directed to:

Independent Commission on Disarmament and Security Issues (ICDSI)
Box 16260
S-103 25 Stockholm
Sweden

Glossary

anti-ballistic missile (ABM) Any missile used to intercept and destroy hostile ballistic missiles, or otherwise neutralize them. Anti-ballistic-missile defence equipment includes weapons, target acquisitions, tracking and guidance radar, plus ancillary installations with the same purpose.

atomic bomb (A-bomb) A weapon based on the rapid fissioning of combinations of selected materials, thereby including an explosion (along with the emission of radiation).

atomic demolition munition (ADM) A nuclear device designed to be detonated on or below the ground surface or under water as a mine against material-type targets to block, deny access, and/or canalize the enemy.

ballistic missile A pilotless projectile propelled into space by one or more rocket boosters. Thrust is terminated at some early stage, after which reentry vehicles follow trajectories that are governed mainly by gravity and aerodynamic drag. Midcourse corrections and terminal guidance permit only minor modifications to the flight path.

battlefield nuclear weapon (BNW) Short-range systems (between 0–150 km), principally artillery and missiles.

cruise missile A guided missile which relies on aerodynamic lift to offset gravity and propulsion to counteract drag; it is in effect a pilotless aircraft. The flight path of a cruise missile remains within the earth's atmosphere.

circular error probable (CEP) A measure of the accuracy of a missile: the radius of the circle around a target within which half of the missiles aimed at the target can be expected to land.

enhanced-radiation weapon (ERW) A weapon, such as the neutron warhead, with high and rapid radiation effects and relatively limited blast effects.

fallout The return to the earth's atmosphere of particles contaminated with radioactive material from a radioactive cloud caused by a nuclear explosion.

forward based system (FBS) The Soviet Union describe these as American nuclear weapons stationed in and around Europe and Asia and capable of striking the Soviet territory.

hydrogen bomb (H-bomb) A nuclear weapon that derives its energy largely from nuclear fusion, triggered by a fission device; a thermonuclear weapon.

intercontinental ballistic missile (ICBM) A land-based rocket-propelled vehicle capable of delivering a warhead to intercontinental ranges (in excess of 5,500 km).

intermediate-range ballistic missile (IRBM) [NATO definition] A rocket with a range between 1,500 and 5,000 km.
    medium-range ballistic missile [Warsaw Pact definition] A rocket with a range between 1,500 and 5,000 km.

kiloton A measure of the yield of a nuclear weapon, equivalent to 1,000 tons TNT. (The Hiroshima bomb had a yield of approximately 13 kilotons.)

launcher That equipment which launches a missile. ICBM launchers are land-based launchers which can be either fixed or mobile. SLBM launchers are the missiles tubes on a ballistic missile submarine. An ASBM launcher is the carrier aircraft with associated equipment. Launchers for cruise missiles can be installed on aircraft, ships or land-based vehicles or installations.

manoeuvrable reentry vehicle (MRV) A ballistic missile warhead or decoy whose accuracy can be improved by terminal guidance mechanisms.

medium-range ballistic missile (MRBM) [NATO definition] A rocket with a range between 150 and 1,500 km.

multiple independently targetable reentry vehicle (MIRV) A missile payload comprising two or more warheads that can engage separate targets. See also **multiple reentry vehicle; reentry vehicle.**

multiple reentry vehicle (MRV) A missile payload comprising two or more warheads that engage the same target. See also **multiple independently targetable reentry vehicle; reentry vehicle.**

national technical means of verification (NTM) Assets that are under national control for monitoring compliance with the provisions of an agreement. NTM include photographic reconnaissance satellites, aircraft-based systems (such as radar and optical systems), as well as sea- and ground-based systems (such as radar and antennae for collecting telemetry).

nuclear munitions A nuclear bomb, shell warhead, or other deliverable ordnance item (as opposed to an experimental device) that explodes as a result of energy released by atomic nuclei by fission, fusion or both.

penetration aid (penaids) Devices employed by offensive weapons systems, such as ballistic missiles and bombers, to increase the probability of penetrating enemy defences.

permissive action links (PAL) Electronic systems for the control of nuclear warheads whereby these can be armed only if positive action to this end is taken by a duly constituted authority, such as the President of the United States or the Supreme Allied Commander, Europe.

post-boost vehicle (PBV) Often referred to as a 'bus' the PBV is that part of a missile payload carrying the reentry vehicles, a guidance package, fuel and thrust devices for altering the ballistic flight path so that the reentry vehicles can be dispensed sequentially towards different targets.

quick reaction alert Readiness procedures designed to reduce reaction times and increase the survivability of tactical aircraft, mainly in the NATO area.

reentry vehicle (RV) The portion of a ballistic missile which carries the nuclear warhead. It is called a reentry vehicle because it reenters the earth's atmosphere in the terminal portion of the missile trajectory.

submarine-launched ballistic missile (SLBM) Any ballistic missile transported by and launched from a submarine. May be short-, medium-, intermediate-, or long-range.

tactical aircraft Land- and carrier-based aircraft designed primarily as general-purpose forces. Selected American elements are routinely assigned strategic nuclear missions.

throw-weight Ballistic missile throw-weight is the useful weight placed on a trajectory towards the target by the boost stages of the missile. For the purposes of SALT II throw-weight is defined as the sum of the weight of (a) the RV or RVs; (b) any PBV or similar devices for releasing or targeting one or more RVs; and (c) any anti-ballistic missile penetration aids, including their release devices.

warheads That part of a missile, projectile, torpedo, rocket or other munition which contains either the nuclear or thermonuclear system, the high-explosive system, the chemical or biological agents, or the inert materials intended to inflict damage.

yield The energy released in an explosion. The energy released in the detonation of a nuclear weapon is generally measured in terms of the kilotons or megatons of TNT required to produce the same energy release (1 kiloton = 1,000 tons of TNT; 1 megaton = 1 million tons of TNT).

References and notes

1 Speech by Admiral of the Fleet the Earl Mountbatten of Burma on the occasion of the award of the Louise Weiss Foundation Prize at Strasbourg on 11 May 1979, p. 6.
2 Estimates vary, but this group typically is said to include: Argentina, Brazil, Iraq, Libya, Pakistan, South Africa, South Korea, and Taiwan. Advanced industrial nations like Canada, the Federal Republic of Germany, Italy, Japan, the Netherlands, Norway, Sweden, and Switzerland also are proficient in nuclear technologies, but have declared that they have no interest in acquiring weapons capabilities and thus are typically not included in this group. A US satellite registered a flash over the South Atlantic in September 1979 that was characteristic of a nuclear explosion. This led many to suspect that South Africa had detonated a nuclear device. However, subsequent analysis by an American board of independent experts concluded that there could be alternative explanations of the satellite's observation, and that the flash did not constitute definite proof of a nuclear explosion.
3 D. F. Ustinov: *Serving the Motherland and the Communist Cause* (Moscow, 1982), p. 72.
4 The US position on these issues is presented most comprehensively in US Department of State Special Report No. 98 (22 March 1982). The Soviet position is presented in a note of the Government of the Union of Soviet Socialist Republics to the Government of the United States of America, reprinted in *Pravda* (6 April 1982).
5 ICDSI Press Statement (14 June 1981).
6 A more detailed description of the effects of nuclear weapons, from which this account has been drawn, can be seen in: *Nuclear Weapons: Report of the Secretary General of the United Nations* (Autumn Books, 1980). Other helpful sources include: US National Academy of Sciences: *Long-Term World Wide Effects of Multiple Nuclear-Weapons Detonations* (1975); US Office of Technology Assessment: *The Effects of Nuclear War* (Washington, 1978), referred to hereafter as 'OTA Study'; and Samuel Glasstone and Philip J. Dolan (eds): *The Effects of Nuclear Weapons*, 3rd edition (GPO, 1977). The previously mentioned article by Jonathan Schell provides a chilling synthesis of these and other sources.
7 Committee for the Compilation of Materials on Damage Caused by

the Atomic Bombs in Hiroshima and Nagasaki: *Hiroshima and Nagasaki: The Physical, Medical, and Social Effects of the Atomic Bombings,* translated by Eisei Ishikawa and David Swain (Hutchinson, 1981).

8 'Effects of Nuclear Attacks, Hiroshima and Nagasaki; Statements to the Independent Commission on Disarmament and Security Issues', (December 1981), pp. 7–8; hereafter 'Testimony'.

9 John Hersey: *Hiroshima* (Alfred Knopf, 1946), p. 33.

10 'Testimony', p. 11.

11 Summary Proceedings of the First Congress of the International Physicians for the Prevention of Nuclear War (20–25 March 1981), p. 5.

12 P. M. S. Blackett: *Studies of War* (Oliver and Boyd, 1962), p. 63. This and subsequent sources are quoted in Jeffrey Record: *US Nuclear Weapons in Europe* (Brookings, 1974).

13 Helmut Schmidt: *Defense or Retaliation?* (Praeger, 1962), p. 101.

14 Alain C. Enthoven and K. Wayne Smith: *How Much Is Enough?* (Harper and Row, 1971), p. 128.

15 Mountbatten, loc. cit.

16 Schell, op. cit.

17 Julian Perry-Robinson: 'Chemical, and Radiological Warfare: Future from the Past', paper prepared for ICDSI (September 1981).

18 Congressman (now Senator) Henry Jackson, US *Congressional Record,* 9 October 1951, 5 June 1952.

19 The information available about the composition of military expenditure is limited and unsatisfactory. Countries publish vastly different amounts of information, in vastly different forms. The use made of available statistics is also inadequate, even in relation to the economic importance of military expenditure in industrial countries. There is little economic analysis of the military sector and its effects on the overall economy. In what follows, statistics for military expenditure are taken from the Stockholm International Peace Research Institute (SIPRI) *Yearbook* for 1982 and earlier years. SIPRI totals vary in some cases from totals given in national sources.

20 Official Soviet sources show a decline in military expenditure as a share of national income from 15.4 per cent in 1950 to 6.5 per cent in 1960, 6.3 per cent in 1970, 4.7 per cent in 1975, 4.4 per cent in 1976, 4.1 per cent in 1977, 4 per cent in 1978 and 3.9 per cent in 1979 ('Narodnoe Khozyastvo SSSR v 1967–1980'; *Pravda,* 24 January 1982).

21 In the United Kingdom, according to official national accounts, the share of military and civilian wages and salaries fell from 48 per cent of military expenditure in 1976 to 42 per cent in 1980. In Japan, the share of 'personnel and provisions' declined from 56 per cent in 1976 to 49 per cent in 1980.

22 Military demand is sharply different from other components of final demand, as detailed studies of 'input/output' relationships for the United States, Canada, France, and the United Kingdom show. While military demand is concentrated in mechanical and electronic goods, non-military public demand is centred in construction and services, and private consumption is distributed across such industries as food, services, housing, motor vehicles, restaurants.

23 Such is the conclusion of the few empirical studies of military employment – which are in general based on input/output information for the US and France in the 1950s and 1960s. See, for example, Wassily Leontief and Marvin Hoffenberg: 'The Economic Impact of Disarmament', *Scientific American*, April 1961, Vol. 204, No. 4, pp. 47–55. These studies, and the discussion which follows, do not take into account 'multiplier' effects associated with expenditures which follow initial outlays as wages and profits earned in military or non-military activities are spent on further consumption.

24 US Department of Labor, Bureau of Labor Statistics: 'Projections of the Post-Vietnam Economy, 1975' (1972).

25 Calculated on the basis of statistics in Jacques Aben: 'Désarmement, Activité et Emploi', in *Défense Nationale*, May 1981, pp. 105–23. France, of course, has a system of national military service with low payments to servicemen. But expenditure on permanent defence personnel alone also created substantially more jobs – 29,240 per billion francs – than expenditure on other military purchases; expenditure on conscripts created over 150,000 jobs per billion francs.

26 Max A. Rutzick: 'Skills and Location of Defense-Related Workers', US Department of Labor: *Monthly Labor Review*, February 1970, pp. 11–16.

27 United Nations General Assembly: Study on the Relationship between Disarmament and Development, A/36/356, 5 October 1981.

28 United Nations General Assembly: Study on the Relationship between Disarmament and Development, A/36/356, 5 October 1981, p. 85.

29 Economic Report of the President, US Government Printing Office, February 1982, p. 86.

30 Ronald P. Smith: 'Military Expenditure and Investment in OECD Countries, 1954–73', *Journal of Comparative Economics* 4, 19–32 (1980).

31 Abraham S. Becker: 'The Burden of Soviet Defense' (RAND, R-2752-AF, October 1981), citing studies of the Soviet economy made at Stanford University.

32 In the US, for example, military purchases in 1972 accounted for 3.3 per cent of total final demand, 5.6 per cent of final demand from goods-producing industries, and 13.6 per cent of final demand from metal

products industries, including mechanical and electronics industries. See Emma Rothschild: 'Military Expenditure and Economic Structure', paper prepared for the Independent Commission on Disarmament and Security Issues.

33 *Technical Change and Economic Policy* (OECD, 1980), pp. 30, 68; *OECD Science and Technology Indicators, Basic Statistical Series,* volume B, January 1982.

34 Soviet experts state that centrally planned economies will be able to reduce such obstacles under different international circumstances.

35 In what follows, China is not included in general discussions of 'developing countries', except where specifically noted.

36 Statistics on arms transfers taken from US Arms Control and Disarmament Agency: *World Military Expenditures and Arms Transfers,* Washington, DC, 1982.

37 Many developing countries spend a higher proportion of military expenditure on procurement than do developed countries. This reflects the fact that wages are generally many times lower in developing countries, while imported weapons cost the same as or even more than in developed countries.

38 Lance Taylor: 'Military Economics in the Third World', paper prepared for the Independent Commission on Disarmament and Security Issues. Taylor's econometric findings call into question a well-known study (Emile Benoit: *Defense and Economic Growth in Developing Countries,* 1973) which on the basis of earlier data for a smaller sample of countries found a positive relationship between defence spending and economic growth.

39 Under such circumstances, increased military spending could also lead to a more unequal distribution of income. People who work in the defence establishment are likely to have relatively high incomes and 'modern' tastes. Their extra demand might be met by diverting capacity and capital formation from industries producing wage goods consumed by less skilled workers and the poor. Demand increases, but as a consequence the distribution of income gets worse.

40 The countries include Austria, Bangladesh, Costa Rica, Fiji, Finland, Hong Kong, Ivory Coast, Jamaica, Japan, Liberia, Luxemburg, Mauritania, Mexico, Nepal, Panama, Sierra Leone, Sri Lanka, and Trinidad.

41 All five nuclear-weapon states have given negative guarantees which in varying terms state that they would not use nuclear weapons first against non-nuclear-weapon states. They follow:

China: 'For the present, all the nuclear countries, particularly the super-Powers, which possess nuclear weapons in large quantities, should immediately undertake not to resort to the threat or use of nuclear weapons against the non-nuclear countries and nuclear-free zones. China is not only ready to undertake this commitment but wishes to reiterate that at no time and in no circumstances will it be the first to use nuclear weapons' (Document of the Ad Hoc Committee of the Tenth Special Session, A/S-10/AC. 1/17, p. 3).

France: 'As regards § 59 concerning assurances of the non-use of nuclear weapons against non-nuclear States, the delegation of France would recall that France is prepared to give such assurances, in accordance with arrangements to be negotiated, to those States which have constituted among themselves non-nuclear zones' (Document of the Tenth Special Session, A/S-10/PV. 27, p. 68).

Soviet Union: 'From the rostrum of the United Nations special session our country declares that the Soviet Union will never use nuclear weapons against those States which renounce the production and acquisition of such weapons and do not have them on their territories' (Document of the Special Session, A/S-10/PV. 5, pp. 28-30).

United Kingdom: 'The United Kingdom is now ready formally to give such an assurance. I accordingly give the following assurance, on behalf of my Government, to non-nuclear-weapon States which are parties to the Non-Proliferation Treaty or to other internationally binding commitments not to manufacture or acquire nuclear explosive devices: Britain undertakes not to use nuclear weapons against such States except in the case of an attack on the United Kingdom, its dependent territories, its armed forces or its allies by such a State in association or alliance with a nuclear-weapon State' (Document of the Special Session, A/S-10/PV. 26, p.4).

United States: 'The United States will not use nuclear weapons against any non-nuclear-weapon State party to the Treaty on the Non-Proliferation of Nuclear Weapons or any comparable internationally binding commitment not to acquire nuclear explosive devices, except in the case of an attack on the United States, its territories or armed forces, or its allies, by such a State allied to a nuclear-weapon State, or associated with a nuclear-weapon State in carrying out or sustaining the attack' (Ad Hoc Committee of the Tenth Special Session, A/S-10/AC. 1/30, p. 1).

42 Istvan Kende: *Local Wars in Asia, Africa, and Latin America, 1945–1969* (Budapest: Centre for Afro-Asian Research of the Hungarian Academy of Sciences, 1972).

43 Giorgi Arbatov called attention to the fact that from the Soviet point of view the whole problem is extremely complicated due to differences in military structures, salaries, prices, etc. This recommendation does not in his view provide an adequate basis for comparison and assessment. The Soviet Union consequently, together with twenty other states, abstained from voting on the resolution in question.